More Laughing Out Loud

MYRON COHEN

MORE
LAUGHING
OUT
LOUD

with drawings by SHEILA GREENWALD

GRAMERCY PUBLISHING COMPANY • NEW YORK

Dedication

TO THE MEMBERS OF THE BOARD OF THE MYRON
COHEN FOUNDATION, WHOSE HELP IS SO GREATLY
APPRECIATED

Copyright © MCMLX *by Myron Cohen*
All rights reserved
Manufactured in the United States of America
Library of Congress Catalog Card Number: 60-16865

This edition published by Gramercy Publishing Company,
a division of Crown Publishers, Inc., by arrangement
with The Citadel Press.
A   B   C   D   E   F   G   H

PREFACE

I began telling stories when I was a silk salesman in the Garment Center and as my friends and associates will attest, I enjoyed it so much that I never stopped.

I told stories to customers, competitors, and cutters, and soon it got to a point where I had a story for every occasion. If someone started talking about his wife, I'd get a gleam in my eye and smile, "Wife . . . Did you hear the one about the new bride who asked her spouse, 'If someone asks me what I see in you, what should I tell him?' " And I'd go on and on and on. . . .

Before long, everyone in the Garment Center began encouraging me to become a professional. My boss said, "You're a wonderful story teller and you ought to get paid for telling them. But not by me!"

And when I left the silk business to become a full-time comedian, there were even more opportunities for me to tell my stories. I told them in night clubs, on TV, at conventions, and I even got around to telling them in print. Writing my first book, *Laughing Out Loud,* was a pleasurable experience, but unfortunately there were too many stories I could not include because of lack of space.

When my publisher suggested that I write a sequel, I welcomed the opportunity to share more of my favorite stories with you.

CONTENTS

Once a Salesman . . .   17

Strictly from Hunger   41

Do Not Disturb   60

Calling All Cards   67

The Cocktail Hour   85

No Place Like Home   107

Caught in the Sports Whirl   132

Tales of Salesmen   151

Katleman's Kapers   173

Hurray for the Irish   186

One for the Road   196

ONCE A SALESMAN...

Some of my most enjoyable afternoons are spent visiting my many friends in the Garment Center. Whenever I appear, I set off a chain reaction. "Hey, Myron," someone will say, "did you hear the one about . . ." and it'll start . . . the stories will begin to fly. Bosses, employees, models, and secretaries all have stories to tell and most of them are worth listening to.

Let's start off with the bosses.

A boss is a fellow who'll raise the roof before he'll raise your salary. He's the guy who shares the credit with the fellow who did the work and the one who watches the clock during the coffee break.

☻

Two cutters were discussing their respective bosses.

"My boss is very cheap and is very unpopular with all his employees," said one.

"My boss," said the other, "you can't help liking him. If you don't, he fires you."

☺

"Do I detect the odor of liquor on your breath?" a stingy boss asked his sales manager.

"You do," admitted the sales manager. "I've just been celebrating the twentieth anniversary of the last raise you gave me."

☺

A guy who noticed that his boss looked pretty unhappy said, "You sure look worried."

"Listen," answered the boss. "I have so many worries that, if something happened today, I wouldn't have time to worry about it for another two weeks."

☺

A. E. Wullschleger, who was my last boss in the Garment Center, received a call from an employment agency about a fellow who worked for him.

"Was he a steady worker?" the fellow from the agency asked.

"Steady?" A. E. screamed. "He was motionless!"

☺

And A. E.'s former junior partner Henry Roth opines that a lot of guys who think their boss is dumb would be out of a job if he were any smarter.

☺

The eagle-eyed owner of a silk firm walked through his shipping department one day and noticed a boy lounging against a box reading a comic book.

"How much do you get a week?" he asked the boy grimly.

"Fifty dollars a week, sir."

The owner handed him fifty dollars out of his pocket and said, "Here's a week's pay. Now get out!"

As the boy left, the angry man turned to the head of the shipping department and snapped, "When did you hire him?"

"Never, sir," was the reply. "He just brought in some packages from another firm and was waiting for his receipt."

If you work hard and keep both feet on the ground, you'll eventually reach a point at which you'll be able to keep both feet on a desk.

A boss approached one of his most ambitious and competent men and told him, "I've had my eye on you. You're a hard worker, and you've put in long hours. You're very ambitious."

"Thank you," replied the employee.

"So, consequently," added the boss, "I'm going to fire you. It's men like you who start competing companies."

A boss who was evaluating the worth of one of his employees said, "I'm overpaying him, but he's worth it."

"Your salary is your personal business," a boss told his newest employee, " and it shouldn't be disclosed to anyone."

"I wouldn't think of mentioning it to anyone," came the reply. "I'm just as much ashamed of it as you are."

My brother Milton of Kay Windsor asked me whether I heard about the nearsighted employee who almost worked himself to death. He never could see when the boss was coming so he had to keep working all the time.

☺

A guy who applied for a job as a resident buyer gave such a glowing account of himself that the boss got suspicious.

"How long did you work in the other place?" he asked.

"Twenty years."

"How old are you?"

"Thirty."

"Then how could you work for twenty years?"

"Overtime."

☺

"Who are you going to get to fill my vacancy?" queried a cutter who had just been fired.

"Sam," growled his erstwhile employer, "you're not leaving any vacancy!"

☺

"Ability," says Jack Silverman of The International, "is what will get you to the top if the boss has no daughter."

☺

PROSPECTIVE EMPLOYEE: Just why do you want a married man to work for you rather than a bachelor?

BOSS: The married men don't get so upset if I yell at them.

☺

A boss's wife tiptoed silently into his office, sneaked behind him while his head was down, clasped her hands over his eyes, and said, "Guess who?"

"I told you there was no time for fooling around," he shouted. "Now get those letters out."

☺

Boss: This is the end. You're fired!
Worker: Fired? I always thought that slaves were sold.

☺

Sign on a Boss's Desk: THIS IS A NON-PROFIT ORGANIZATION
PLEASE HELP US CHANGE

☺

Henny Youngman says his unemployed brother-in-law gave up his job because of illness. His boss got sick of him.

☺

The fiery-tempered boss of a silk firm returned to his office after a month's vacation in Florida and was approached by a timid bookkeeper.

"If you don't mind, Mr. Kramer," said the bookkeeper meekly, "I'd like to take my vacation now."

"I was away for four weeks," snarled Mr. Kramer. "Wasn't that enough?"

☺

"No man goes before his time," says New York *Mirror* scribe Frances Merron. "Unless, of course, the boss leaves early."

☺

A boss told his junior partner, "Quite a few people in this firm are already working a four-day week. The only trouble is that it takes them five days to do it."

☺

The prospective boss looked up at the job applicant and asked, "Tell me, what have you done?"

"Me?" answered the startled applicant. "About what?"

☺

A cutter was handed a pay envelope which, by error, contained a blank check. Astonished, he looked at it and moaned, "Just what I thought would happen. My deductions finally caught up with my salary!"

☺

When the firm's top buyer who happened to be a woman asked the boss for a raise, he objected.

"Your salary is already higher than any male buyer working here and they all have families with two and three kids."

"Look," she countered, "I thought we got paid for what we produce *here*, not for what we produce at home on our own time."

☺

Did you hear about the fellow who was so in love with his wife that he went home for all his coffee breaks?

☺

The fellow who said, "The surest way to get a thing done is to give it to the busiest man you know, and he'll have his secretary do it," knew what he was talking about. You can't underestimate the value of a good secretary. I knew one employer who spent three months looking for a suitable secretary because he knows it pays to have a good head on your shoulder.

☺

I like the story about the boss who told his new secretary, "Renee, always add a column of figures at least three times before you show me the result."

The next day she came in with a broad smile. "Mr. Drew," she said, "I added these figures ten times."

"Good," he said. "I like a girl to be thorough."

"And here," she said, "are the ten answers."

☺

And then there was the girl who graduated from secretarial school with highest honors. She finished three laps ahead of her closest competition.

☺

A businessman hired a new secretary, and the first morning she worked for him, he dictated a letter to his wife who was away on a trip. When she brought the letter back for his signature, it was perfect with one exception. She had omitted his final words which were, "I love you."

"Did you forget my last sentence?" he asked.

"Why, no," she replied. "I didn't think you were dictating."

☺

A businessman had to fire his secretary because she lacked experience. All she knew was shorthand and typing.

☺

A secretary who was leaving for her annual vacation told her replacement, "While I'm gone you'll continue what I was working on, but that doesn't include Mr. Franklin."

☺

The personnel director who was checking the references of a prospective secretary called her former boss.

"How long did she work for you?" he questioned.

"About eight hours," said the former boss.

"But she told me she was with you for three years."

The ex-boss replied, "She was! She was!"

☺

"Most amazing," the boss said to his new secretary. "You've been with us only two weeks and already you're a month behind in your work."

☺

"Just why are you so suspicious of your husband's secretary?"

"Because I used to be a secretary."

☺

It's Jimmy Durante's story about the boss who dictated a difficult letter to his secretary. When she brought it back for his signature, he read a garbled version of his carefully thought-out remarks.

"Didn't you read this letter before you put it on my desk?" he screamed.

"Oh, no," she answered. "I thought it was confidential."

☺

A girl asked her friend, "How long did your sister work for her last boss?"

Her friend replied, "Until she got him."

☺

One afternoon the boss's wife met him at the office. As they were going down the elevator, it stopped, and a shapely and extremely pretty secretary got on. Poking the boss in the ribs, she said, "Hello, cutie pie!"

Without blinking an eyelash, the wife leaned over with a smile and said, "I'm Mrs. Pie."

NEW SECRETARY: How long have you been working here?
OLD SECRETARY: Ever since the boss threatened to fire me.

Phil Foster knew a very efficient secretary. She didn't miss a coffee break in twenty-five years.

"The average secretary's life is divided into two parts," says King Features' columnist Mel Heimer. "The first part is spent

listening to a boss who dictates, and the second is spent dictating to a husband who listens."

A boss called his new secretary into his office.

"Miss Handler," he said, "you're the best-looking girl we ever had working in this office."

A pleased look came into her eyes.

"You're a smart dresser. You have a pleasant voice, and you make a good impression on my customers," the boss continued.

"Oh, thank you," she said. "Your compliments are very pleasing."

"Enjoy them to the fullest," said the boss, "because now we're going to discuss your spelling, punctuation, and typing."

☺

A secretary was complaining to a friend, "If it weren't for the good salary, the air conditioning, the swimming pool, the free theatre tickets, the four-week vacations, and the generous pension and profit-sharing plans, I swear I'd quit this miserable job!"

☺

A boss told his secretary, "Congratulations, Miss Arnold. This is the earliest you've ever been late."

☺

Jim O'Connor, the popular night club editor of the New York *Journal-American*, likes the story of the harassed boss who told a friend at lunch, "My secretary has an unusual brain."

"Unusual brain?" asked his friend.

"Yes, it starts working the moment she gets up in the morning and doesn't stop 'til she gets to my office."

☺

Two secretaries were talking.

"How's your boss?" asked one.

"Oh, he's all right except he's kind of bigoted," said the other.

"Why?"

"He thinks words can only be spelled one way."

☻

A tardy secretary told her boss, "I'm really not late. I took my coffee break coming in."

☻

Charlie Dawn of the Chicago *American* tells of the young secretary who informed her boss she was quitting.

"But why?" he questioned.

"Because I don't like the surroundings," she replied.

"What exactly don't you like?" he asked.

"You!"

☻

Anyone who likes to listen to good stories knows that many of the funniest yarns deal with the lives and experiences of the Garment Center manufacturers.

I like the story of the unsuccessful manufacturer, known for his ill-fated ventures, who consulted a psychiatrist after having the same dream for twenty-five nights in succession.

"In my dream," he told the head doctor, "there are always two of me. We're seated in chairs facing each other, and one of me is giving advice to the other me. Doctor, am I losing my mind?"

"No," replied the psychiatrist. "As long as you just dream you're all right. But if you listen to that advice . . . you're *sunk!*"

☻

Two coat manufacturers were exchanging gripes.

"You should see my showroom," said one. "It's like a haunted house."

"Don't complain," said the other. "You're lucky to have ghosts."

☻

Jack Geizler, one of my former bosses, claims many manufacturers don't know where the next check is coming from or when the last one is coming back.

☺

A nouveau riche manufacturer hired a researcher to trace his pedigree. A few weeks later, a friend who knew about the researcher asked about the results. "He uncovered so much," the manufacturer said, "that now I'm paying him hush money."

☺

Claire Barry and husband Al Weinberg heard a prosperous man being discussed by two rivals.

"He claims he was born with a gold spoon in his mouth," said one.

"If he was," said the other nastily, "I'll bet there was somebody else's initials on it!"

☺

A manufacturer was reprimanding his son for being lazy. "Son," he said, "when I was your age, I worked sixteen hours a day learning the silk business."

"I'm very proud of you, father," replied the son. "If it hadn't been for your ambition and perseverance, I might have had to do something like that myself!"

☺

The story is told of the eighty-five-year-old manufacturer who was known for his penny pinching.

"Can't you persuade him," a friend told his wife, "that he can't take it with him?"

The wife replied, "Why, I can't even persuade him that someday he will have to go."

☺

A cutter who noticed that the head bookkeeper hadn't been to work for a few days asked a member of the bookkeeping department, "Has Mr. Lewis gone away to take a rest?"

"No," replied the bookkeeper. "He's gone away to avoid it."

☺

Did you hear about the wealthy Garment Center executive who was so ostentatious he told his wife to bury him in Miami when he died?

☺

Speaking about departed manufacturers, I like Harry Hershfield's tale of the owner of a silk business who insisted on having all his checks dated ahead. When he died his tombstone read: HERE LIES SAM JONES. DIED JUNE 5TH AS OF JULY 1ST.

☺

And then there's the story of the partners who arrived at a cemetery to bid good-bye to a competitor and couldn't find his grave.

"Maybe," said one, "he put it in his wife's name."

☺

A fellow who worked in the Garment Center met his ex-boss's wife. She looked very radiant and extremely happy.

"Mrs. Stein," he said, "you must have some good news. You seem to be bursting with it."

"Wonderful news!" she exclaimed. "Simply wonderful news. My husband's had a breakdown, and we have to go to Palm Springs for the next three months."

☺

In a similar vein, here's a conversation I recently overheard between two manufacturers. The first said, "I just spent a two-week vacation in Pallum Springs."

"Speak English for a change," the other said. "You mean Palm Springs."

"You're right," the first one replied. "It was my error. I had it confused with Pallum Beach."

☺

An efficiency expert was called in to see why a Seventh Avenue firm was losing money.

"What do you do around here?" he asked one fellow.

"Nothing," was the reply.

"And you?" he asked, directing his question at another member of the company.

"Nothing at all," the second man responded.

"Hmmmm," said the efficiency expert knowingly, "just as I thought. Too much duplication."

☺

And while we're on the subject, how about the one Monica Boyar told me of the woman who was explaining her husband's job to a friend? "My husband's an efficiency expert for a large company," she said.

"What's an efficiency expert?" her companion asked.

"Well, put it this way," the spouse explained. "If we women did it, they'd call it nagging."

☺

After ordering 15,000 dresses from a manufacturer, a buyer asked, "How long will it be before you deliver them?"

"Thirty days," said the manufacturer.

"Thirty days," protested the buyer. "Why the good Lord took only six days to create the entire world."

"That may be true," said the manufacturer, "but have you

taken a good look at it lately?"

Sign on a shuttered Seventh Avenue store: WE UNDERSOLD
EVERYONE.

The nouveau riche manufacturer and his spouse were having difficulty adjusting to a life of elegance. After the first dinner in their new twenty-five room mansion, the husband turned to his wife and asked, "Do you want to have an after dinner drink in the library?"

"It's too late," she replied. "The library closes at six."

While selling a friend a new suit, a Seventh Avenue clothier was raving about the garment. "It's beautiful," he said. "Even your best friends won't recognize you in that suit! Just take a walk outside for a minute and examine it in the light."

The customer friend went out and returned a moment later. The clothier rushed up to him with a smile.

"Good afternoon, stranger," he beamed. "What can I do for you?"

Mike Durso related the story of a businessman who was telling his friend about the host of worries plaguing him, declaring, "They're beginning to smother me, dozens closing in from all sides."

"Thing for you to do," counseled the friend, "is to simplify them by lumping the related ones. That's what I did, and now I have only three problems—nagging creditors, a profitless business, and the fact I'm broke."

A businessman told a friend, "I wanted my son to share in the business, but the government beat him to it."

☺

A successful, but illiterate manufacturer who had managed for years by signing his checks with two X's received a call from his bank.

"One of your checks came in today," a teller told him, "and it was signed with three X's. Is it yours or is it a forgery?"

"It's mine," explained the manufacturer. "You see, my wife has social ambitions and she thinks I ought to have a middle name."

☺

A teacher asked a Garment Center manufacturer's son, "How many seasons are there?"

The boy thought for a moment and then said, "Just two."

"What are they?" inquired the puzzled teacher.

"Slack and busy."

☺

Robert Dana, of the New York *World-Telegram and Sun* knew a very poor businessman. He went bankrupt twice and didn't make a cent either time.

☺

A guy described a pair of dishonest businessmen.

"They're so crooked that, if one stood at the top of a circular staircase and the other at the bottom, they could look each other in the eye."

☺

COLE (over the phone): Are you going to pay us?

RUSSELL: Not just yet.

COLE: If you don't, I'll tell all your other creditors that you paid us.

☺

Bob and Phil decided to end their partnership and go their separate ways. Since each knew the other was planning to start a new business of his own, a bitter rivalry developed during the last days over who would retain the services of Stone the designer.

Bob returned from lunch one day and saw the designer and Phil talking in Phil's office. He waited outside until Stone walked out and then stopped him.

"How much did that cheap chiseler offer you?" Bob demanded.

"Why, nothing," replied the surprised Stone.

"Don't take it," roared Bob. "I'll give you double."

☺

"In the old days," observes Jack Benny, "a man was known by the company he kept. Nowadays, he's known by the one he merges."

☺

Seven prominent members of the Garment Center were named pallbearers in the will of a manufacturer who died penniless and owing them considerable sums. "They have been wonderful creditors," the will said, "and I would like to have them carry me to the end."

☺

A manufacturer told his newest employee, "All I had when I first faced the cold business world was youth, determination, and

33

a will that left me a quarter of a million dollars."

☺

"On Seventh Avenue," notes writer Paul Denis, "when people don't care for something, they say, 'It's not my glass of tea.'"

☺

Fred and Jim were both wealthy. They were also business rivals and disliked each other intensely. At every opportunity each flaunted his wealth in the other's face.

One day when they met, Fred said, "Listen Jim, I can buy and sell you."

"Is that so," answered Jim. "I not only can buy you, but I can afford to keep you."

☺

Did you hear about the pickpocket who's reading the fashion pages because he wants to see where the pockets will be next season?

☺

A manufacturer stepped briskly up to the proprietor of a swank men's shop. "I just found out," he said, "that my son has owed you for a suit of clothes for three years."

"That's right," said the proprietor. "Did you come in to settle the account?"

"No," said the manufacturer. "I'd like a suit on the same terms."

☺

"It's not easy to get ahead in this world," a businessman assured a young friend. "As a lad I started out at the bottom. I struggled, worked, sweated, climbing the ladder of life hand over hand, rung by rung."

"And now," interposed the friend, "you are a great success?"

"Well, no," admitted the businessman, "but I'm getting good at climbing ladders!"

☺

There's a manufacturer who lost a fortune in the stock market and now won't even read a book with margins in it.

☺

A labor leader who was seeking a wife went to a matrimonial agency. "Is this a union shop?" he inquired. Assured that it was, he picked out a picture of a luscious twenty-three-year-old and said, "I'll take her."

"No, you have to take this lady," said the manager, showing a picture of a gray haired woman of sixty.

"Why do I have to take her?" thundered the labor leader.

"She," said the manager, "has seniority."

☺

"It won't be long until we all have money to burn," says Sidney Fields of the New York *Mirror*. "In fact, it's almost cheaper than fuel right now."

☺

A manufacturer who refused to give a buyer his price and lost a sale said, "He's the toughest buyer I have to deal with. He not only demands a tooth for a tooth, he expects yours to have gold in it."

☺

Successful partners in business, Steve and Don spent most of their spare time trying to outdo each other. If one bought a $150 suit, the other bought one costing $200. If one bought a Cadillac, the other bought a Rolls Royce.

One day, Steve had a phone put in his car. Don was furious when he heard about it and immediately had one installed in his car. Then he called Steve and said nonchalantly, "This is Don. I'm phoning your car from my car."

"Would you mind holding on for a minute?" answered Steve briskly. "I've got a call on another wire."

A holdup man entered a Seventh Avenue fabric house and ordered the bookkeeper to hand over the payroll.

"I'm very sorry," said the bookkeeper, "but I'm off duty and the union won't let me."

☺

Sid Edwards, the Maître d' at the International, was told of a psychiatrist who caters to the garment trade. He's experimenting with a new form of shock treatment for his wealthier patients.

He sends them his bill in advance.

☺

A wealthy manufacturer who was asked if he'd ever had ulcers replied, "I don't get ulcers. I give them!"

☻

Jackie Gleason tells the story about the businessman who went to a medical specialist, had a check up, and received a bill for $150.

"Your fee is entirely out of line," he complained to the doctor. "Anyway, business is so bad now that I just couldn't afford to pay you that amount."

"All right," said the M.D., "make it $100."

"That's still too much. Even though I'm not making so much now, I still have a wife and five kids to feed."

"Okay," said the doctor, "make it $50."

This went on until the fee was down to $5.

"Look," said the specialist, "you know I'm a leading specialist and have to charge high prices. Why did you come to me in the first place?"

"Where my health is concerned," replied the businessman, "I never stint on money."

☻

A manufacturer who was considering joining a lodge asked the president of one of them, "Does your lodge have any death benefits?"

"It certainly does," the lodge president replied. "When you die, you don't have to pay any more dues."

☻

Steve Allen tells of the spendthrift who was reprimanding his partner for being so frugal.

"Max," he said, "I think the practice of putting something away for a rainy day is foolish."

"That may be so," replied Max, "but that's exactly what Noah's neighbors used to say when he was building his ark."

☺

A manufacturer who wanted to borrow $250,000 went to his bank.

"That's a lot of money," said the bank president. "Can you give me a statement?"

"Yes," said the manufacturer. "I'm optimistic."

☺

"If it takes two to make a bargain," asks Frank Quinn, of the New York *Mirror*, "how come only one gets it?"

☺

Hal Boyle, the A.P. scribe, likes the story about the Garment Center manufacturer who died and went to heaven. When he arrived at the Holy Gate, he noticed a group of marching angels.

"Do you wish to enter?" asked the guard at the gate.

"I thought I did," replied the man from Seventh Avenue pointing to the marching angels, "but after seeing them, I'm not sure."

"Why?"

"In my entire lifetime I never passed a picket line, and I don't intend to start now."

☺

Georgia Gilly tells of two shady businessmen, known to do most anything for a buck, who were discussing their problems.

"Did the insurance company come up with the fire insurance you asked for?" questioned one.

"No," the other replied. "They offered to give me earthquake insurance instead, but I turned them down."

38

"I don't blame you," the first one agreed. "It's awfully hard to start a convincing earthquake."

☺

"Now, gentlemen," the owner of a big dress house said as he looked around the conference table at his staff. "I have a suggestion to make about a change in company policy for the coming year." Smiling paternally at the men, he continued, "I'd like your opinions, all of you. Those opposed to my little idea will signify by saying, 'I resign'."

☺

A businessman who was supposed to marry his pretty model told her, "Darling, I'm ruined. My business has failed and I'll have to declare bankruptcy. I don't have a cent."

The model replied, "Don't worry, sweetheart. I'll always love you, even if I never see you again."

☺

Speaking about models, I like the tale about the one who went to a cosmetic salon and asked for some advice on highlighting her face.

"If you want to highlight your face," she was advised, "don't wear such tight dresses."

☺

"I don't know the style or color of shoes, but I want low heels," the tall blonde model told the clerk.

"To wear with what?"

"A short, plump, elderly manufacturer."

☺

A manufacturer described his leading model: "She's got the kind of figure you give the once-over twice."

☺

A model was telling how embarrassing it was when her brassiere broke in the middle of a fashion show.

"It was a good thing for me," she said, "that another model was wearing it at the time."

☺

And as any businessman will tell you, we all know thousands of ways to spend money but only one way to make it.

STRICTLY FROM HUNGER

A balanced meal in a restaurant is one from which the diner has a fifty-fifty chance of recovery. I think this is a conservative figure because, when I began as a silk salesman, I ate in places where there was absolutely no chance of recovery.

I can recall one time when I was traveling down South and stopped off for a quick breakfast in an all-night diner.

"A couple of scrambled eggs," I said.

"Comin' right up," said the counterman.

"I'd appreciate it if they were fresh country eggs," I added.

"Yes, sir."

After a couple of mouthfuls I turned to him and said, "My good man! These eggs are terrible! I thought you said they came from the country."

"Yes, sir," he said, "the old country."

☺

A little Jewish fellow entered a restaurant, studied the menu, and asked the waiter how much a roast beef sandwich cost. The waiter told him. Then he looked at the menu again and asked the price of a pastrami sandwich. Again, the waiter told him. Looking at the menu for a third time, the customer asked, "How much is a ham sandwich?"

Before the waiter could answer, the heavens let loose a tremendous clap of thunder and lightning. The little man fell to his knees and directed his terror-filled eyes to the sky. "All right! All right!" he pleaded. "I was only asking!"

☺

One of my favorite restaurants is the Stage Delicatessen. It's hosted by Max Asnas, a portly, good-natured, little man who is often referred to as the Cornbeef Confuscius.

Recently, a customer phoned Max and said, "I'd like to make reservations for six people and six fried herrings." Max replied, "Come right down. I can seat the herrings immediately, but the people will have to wait an hour."

Once, I asked Max why he didn't have a parking lot at his restaurant. He snorted, "If I had a parking lot, I wouldn't need a restaurant!"

☺

A fellow entered a restaurant and sat down at one of the tables. The waiter came and asked him what he would like.

The customer replied, "I'll have two bad eggs on a burnt piece of toast."

"But, sir," said the waiter, "you can't have that here. This is a highly respectable restaurant."

"I can't help that," the customer answered. "I've got worms and anything's good enough for them!"

☺

Mike Grieg of the San Francisco *Examiner* tells of a wealthy Texan who tipped a waiter $100 in a Chicago restaurant.

"Pardon me," gasped the astonished waiter, "I think you've made a mistake."

"That should teach you a lesson," barked the Texan. "Next time I come, I hope I'll get some better service."

☺

One of the women at the restaurant table was unable to finish the big steak she had ordered, so she got a bright idea.

Summoning the waiter, she asked if he would wrap the left-over piece for her dog, explaining to her companions when he had gone, "I haven't got a dog, but now I can have a steak sandwich for my lunch tomorrow."

A few minutes later the accommodating waiter returned with a big paper bag. "I found a lot of pieces of steak left over on other plates," he said, "so I just wrapped them all together."

☺

DINER: Why do you call this an enthusiastic stew?
WAITER: Because the cook put everything he had into it.

☺

Herb Caen of the San Francisco *Chronicle* tells the story of the wealthy Park Avenue socialite who was dining in a Broadway restaurant when it was held up. With methodical precision the stick-up men went from one table to another scooping up all the valuables belonging to the guests. When they reached the socialite's table, one of the crooks noticed her sparkling ring. He walked over, studied it for a moment, and then said, "It's a phony—a piece of glass." Furious, the socialite screamed, "You obviously don't know the first thing about jewelry. This ring costs $15,000." "O.K.," said the crook, "have it your way. Let's have the ring."

☺

A sea food restaurant was stuck with loads of lobster from the previous weeks. "Push lobster," ordered the manager. "No matter what the customers want, recommend lobster."

A few minutes later a man walked in. "What do you suggest?" he asked.

"Well," said the waiter, "the spoiled lobster is very good."

I was dining in Lindy's one evening with my wife, Miriam, when I was introduced to another diner by a mutual friend. We became engrossed in conversation and when I mentioned how much traveling I do, he said, "Well, I, also, do quite a bit of traveling. In fact, I've moved seven times in the past nine years."

I thought for a moment and then said, "Well, I guess you must be either a minister or an army officer."

"No," he shook his head. "I'm neither. I'm a football coach."

Once, when I had an appointment to meet a friend in Lindy's, I parked my car in front of a hydrant. After meeting my acquaintance, I told him that I might leave for a few minutes during the meal to find a safe parking place. After having a plate of soup, I excused myself and went out to my car. However, I was too late. When I arrived, a policeman was writing out a ticket. He looked up at me. "Hey," he said. "You're Myron Cohen. You're my wife's favorite comedian. She's been a big admirer of yours for years."

"Oh, really?" I said. "Does this mean you're not going to give me a ticket?"

"No, it doesn't," the cop said. "Yesterday, my wife sued me for divorce."

A Hollywood agent was seated in a corner at Danny's Hide-A-Way bemoaning his fate.

"What's wrong?" asked a friend.

"It's that new client of mine," groaned the agent. "How'd you like to represent a client that sings like Crosby, wiggles like Presley, fights like John Wayne, and acts like Marlon Brando?"

"Are you crazy?" asked the friend. "You don't have any worries. You'll make a million with this guy."

"Guy nothing, you dope," griped the agent. "It's a girl."

☻

Two Garment Center manufacturers were dining at Sid Allen's Steak Pit and discussing their favorite subject.

"There are hundreds of ways to make a fortune," said one, "but there's only one honest way."

"And what's that?" demanded the other.

"Aha," smiled the first, "I thought you wouldn't know!"

☻

DINER: You call this creamed lobster your special? I can find neither cream nor lobster in it.

WAITER: Yes, sir. That's what makes it special.

☻

A fellow walked into a restaurant and ordered kidneys. While he was waiting for his order, he decided to go next door to a bar and have a few drinks. He forgot about his food and continued to drink. About a half hour later, the waiter from the restaurant came in and told him, "Your kidneys are spoiling."

The customer replied, "I've suspected that for years but I didn't realize it was visible to the naked eye."

☻

Sign in a Chinese restaurant: FORTUNE COOKIES!
DIRE PREDICTIONS, 25¢ EXTRA!

☺

A rabbit and a lion entered a restaurant and parked themselves at the counter. "One head of lettuce," ordered the rabbit. "No dressing." The waiter pointed to the lion. "What'll your friend have?" he asked.

"Nothing."

"What's the matter? Isn't he hungry?"

The rabbit looked him squarely in the eye. "Look," he said, "if this lion was hungry, do you think I'd be sitting here?"

☺

Joey Bishop, the popular young comic, had a very unusual experience recently. He says he sat in the Four Seasons for ten minutes without hearing anyone remark, "This place is a gold mine."

☺

Gene DeForrest of the San Francisco *News-Call Bulletin* likes this one:

A friend called a Madison Avenue advertising executive one afternoon at one o'clock and was told by his secretary, "He's out to lunch, but I'll bet he'll be back soon."

"How do you know?"

"Because nobody took him."

☺

Ivan Paul of the San Francisco *Examiner* applauded when I told him this one:

A fellow who had been waiting over an hour for his lunch

called the waitress over and asked, "Must I sit here until I starve?"

"Oh no," replied the waitress. "We close at six o'clock."

☺

☺

I was seated in a restaurant recently when I heard a customer tell the proprietor, "That fellow who just left was wearing my new coat. Why didn't you say something?"

"As a matter of fact," said the owner, "I did comment to the cashier that the sleeves were too short."

☺

SALESMAN: When is the best time to see Mr. Brown?

RECEPTIONIST: Hard to say. Before lunch he's grouchy,, and after lunch he has indigestion.

☺

The story is told of the owner of a large chain of restaurants who went over his books and discovered that his most trusted employee had stolen over a million dollars from the firm.

"I want no scandal," the owner said. "I'll just fire you and forget about the entire matter."

The employee replied. "So you're going to fire me. True, I robbed your concern of quite a tidy sum. I now have yachts, a country mansion, a town house, jewelry, and every luxury you can think of. I don't need a thing, so why hire somebody else and have him start from scratch?"

☺

Merna Barry and husband Manny Pine overheard two women, seated in a restaurant, who were engrossed in a deep discussion about food.

"What is the opposite of a gourmet?" asked one.

The other replied, "Anyone who has had to live with one for years."

☺

Toots Shor, whose new restaurant may be open by the time this book is published, had a lot of free time when his first restaurant closed. A travel agent submitted an itinerary of a proposed trip around the world. At first Toots thought it a good idea but, when he took a look at the names, he reneged. "I can't pronounce the names of all those places," he said. "What's the use of goin' anywhere if I can't tell people where I've been."

☺

"We guarantee we can fill any order you ask for," boasted the sign outside the new restaurant, "or we'll give you $1,000."

Going inside a wily customer ordered walrus ears on a bun. Sure enough, after five minutes the waiter came back with a $1,000 bill.

"Aha," said the diner, "no walrus ears, you fraud. Take down your sign!"

The waiter slowly shook his head. "It's not the walrus ears. We have plenty of them. We just ran out of buns!"

☺

Jim Walls of the San Francisco *Chronicle* tells of the two diners who were talking. "I hear the owner of this restaurant has hired an ex-actor for cashier," said one.

"Why?" asked the other. "Is he good at juggling figures?"

"No, but he used to be a quick-change artist!"

☺

And at the next table, two men were discussing their wives. "If I had a wife like yours," said one, "I wouldn't go out at night."

"If you had a wife like mine," replied the other, "you wouldn't dare!"

☺

"Waiter," said the irate diner, "you have to take this hash back. It tastes funny."

"I wouldn't be surprised," replied the waiter. "You should have heard the cook laughing while he was making it."

☺

When he heard that a rival restaurant had burned down, a restaurant owner said, "I'm sorry to hear about it, but it's the first time the food's been hot in his place."

☺

I was dining in Lindy's when Harry Richman came in and told me he had just returned from a funeral.

"Oh, I'm sorry to hear that," I said. "Who died?"

"James Mason's cat."

"James Mason's cat?"

"Yes," Harry said tearfully. "Everybody was there and Georgie Jessel delivered a beautiful eulogy. You know, Myron, until I heard Georgie, I never realized how much a cat could do for Israel."

☺

WAITER: There hasn't been much stirring around this restaurant.

DINER: Why not?

WAITER: Somebody stole all the spoons.

☺

Charles Einstein of the San Francisco *Examiner* likes this one:

"I thought this place was under new management, but I see the same manager is still here."

"Yes, sir, but he got married yesterday."

☺

I was dining at Hy Kugler's Satellite Restaurant one evening when I spotted a guest who seemed to have an insatiable appetite.

"Who is that fellow?" I asked Hy.

"Why he's the Russian ambassador to the United States," Hy informed me.

"You know he eats like there's no tomorrow," I said.

"Maybe," said Hy, "he knows something."

☺

George Mitchell, of the Assembly Restaurant tells of the practical joker who sent a collect telegram to a friend which said: I AM PERFECTLY WELL.

About a week later the joker received a heavy package on which he was required to pay considerable charges. Upon opening it, he found a big block of concrete on which was pasted this message: THIS IS THE WEIGHT YOUR TELEGRAM LIFTED FROM MY MIND.

☺

Jerry Sager, Advertising and Publicity Director of the Moss Theatres, overheard this one:

"Waiter," said a diner who had just sampled his dinner, "these veal chops don't seem very tender to me."

"Sir," replied the waiter, "I used to be a butcher, and I can tell you that, less than a month ago, these chops were chasing after a cow."

"That may be," replied the man, "but not for milk!"

☺

DINER: Do you serve crabs?
WAITER: What'll you have? We serve everybody.

☺

American Weekly scribe Joe McCarthy likes this one:
A loudmouthed customer kept shouting at a pretty waitress. Another fellow, who was seated at the opposite end of the dining room, asked the girl, "Do you want me to take care of him for you?"

"Oh, no," she smiled. "He's my husband."

"Husband? But I don't understand."

"It's like this," she explained. "We've got it down to a science. He makes all the other customers feel sorry for me and they give extra large tips."

☺

I was leaving The Old Homestead one evening when I was stopped by a bum who said he needed carfare because he had lost all his money in a card game. "Are you a poker player?" I asked. "No," he said, "but I just left four guys who are."

☺

Charles Schlaifer claims he saw this sign in a restaurant:
OUR STEAKS ARE SO TENDER WE WONDER HOW THE COW
EVER WALKED

☺

A restaurant patron demanded restitution for a topcoat that had been lifted.

"I'm sorry," said the cashier, "but you see the sign says we are not responsible for coats unless checked."

"I know," said the customer, "but my coat was checked."

☺

Jack E. Leonard, the portly one, observes, "The man who reaches for the lunch check has many admirable qualities. He's generous, friendly, and on an expense account."

☺

When a pretty waitress came to work one night, the manager met her at the door.

"Betty," he said, "I want you to put on your cutest uniform,

fix your hair lovely, and see that your make-up is on neat."

"Something special on?" she asked.

"No," he said. "The beef's tough."

☺

A woman arranged a party for her daughter at a restaurant and asked the owner if the comedian who would perform had ever appeared on TV.

"No," he said.

"That's good," replied the woman. "My daughter knows all the TV comics' routines."

☺

Two women entered a restaurant, and one noticed a familiar face at the other end of the room.

"Do you see who I see sitting over there," she said looking where the other woman was sitting. "It's Helen. Tell me, do you believe that terrible story about her?"

"Yes," replied her friend eagerly. "What is it?"

☺

At a restaurant during the breakfast hour, a man asked a waitress for the lone piece of dried-up French toast left in the warming tray. She refused to give it to him, telling him that a fresh batch would be along in a minute. He replied that he would take it anyhow. The waitress, adamant, insisted that he wait for a fresh piece.

"Look lady," he shouted. "If I wanted to fight for breakfast I would have stayed home!"

☺

"How much are the cigars?" asked a customer.

"Two for a quarter," the girl behind the counter said.

"I'll take one."

"That'll be fifteen cents."

The customer paid the money and left. A man who had overheard the transaction came up to the counter. "Here's a dime," he said. "Give me the other one."

☺

Louis Sobol, the New York *Journal-American* columnist, was dining in a restaurant and told the waiter he wanted a baked apple.

"I'm sorry," said the waiter. "We don't have any."

Louis ate in the same restaurant the next three days and each time got the same reply. Finally, on the fourth day, he confronted the waiter and asked, "If you don't have baked apples why do you keep them on the menu?"

The waiter replied, "Would it be better if we left an empty space?"

☺

A pessimist explained why he always dines in restaurants where music is provided.

"Sometimes the music helps me forget the food. And sometimes the food helps me forget the music."

☺

When a restaurant patron complained that his breakfast sausages had meat at one end but bread crumbs at the other, the manager explained it was a matter of expediency. "In these times of rising costs, nobody can make both ends meat."

☺

After receiving a disappointing tip from an extremely crabby customer a waiter told him, "Now I'll give *you* a tip. Don't ever dare to sit at one of my tables again."

☺

A fellow named Ginsberg who was crossing the Atlantic for the first time was assigned to a table with a debonair Frenchman.

The first night out at dinner, the Frenchman rose, bowed politely, and said, "Bon appétit."

Ginsberg bowed politely and said, "Ginsberg."

The next morning at breakfast, the next noon at lunch, and the next evening at dinner, the ceremony was repeated, and Ginsberg felt his politeness wearing a little thin.

"It's getting on my nerves," he told a companion in the lounge. "He tells me his name, Bon Appétit. I tell him my name, Ginsberg. But at the next meal we start all over again."

His friend laughed. "The Frenchman isn't introducing himself. 'Bon appétit' is French for 'I hope you have a pleasant meal.'"

Ginsberg breathed a sigh of relief. The next morning when he appeared at breakfast, the Frenchman was already seated. Ginsberg bowed politely and said, "Bon appétit."

Whereupon the Frenchman rose, bowed, and answered, "Ginsberg."

☺

HOLDUP MAN TO CASHIER IN A CHINESE RESTAURANT: Give me all your money.

CASHIER: To take out?

☺

A waitress who became completely fed up with a patron's unreasonable demands told him, "If I were your wife, I'd give you poison."

"If you were my wife," he said, "I'd take it!"

☺

Sign in a restaurant. IT'S TOUGH TO PAY $2 FOR A STEAK AND IT'S TOUGHER WHEN YOU PAY $1.

☺

Al Kelly and his charming wife dropped into a neighborhood restaurant which both of them agreed was horrible.

"The food was so bad," Al reported later, "we might as well have eaten at home!"

☺

There's a waiter at a certain New York restaurant who is ready to commit suicide. For the last few weeks he's been throwing the tablecloth doodles of a steady customer into the laundry. The other day, the maitre d' pointed out the customer and said, "That's Salvador Dali, the artist."

☺

A fellow looked extremely unhappy when he came home from work one night.

"What's the matter with you?" asked his wife.

"I was in a restaurant this afternoon and I had an argument with a waiter. He got so mad that he called me a pig!"

"Listen," said his wife. "With the price of pork what it is today, you don't have to feel insulted."

☺

Six Sioux Chiefs, waiting for a luncheon table at a restaurant, were asked by the hostess, "Do you have a reservation?" "Yup," said one, "in South Dakota."

☺

A diner at a very exclusive restaurant was puzzled when he noticed that there was water in every ash tray.

"Do you put water in the ash trays to extinguish cigarets more easily?" he asked.

"Partly that, sir," replied the waiter. "But it also keeps people from pocketing them for souvenirs."

☺

I was dining in Shine's one evening with Jim O'Connor, the popular New York *Journal-American* scribe when he told me this story.

An elderly, overweight man visited a doctor. He was examined and put on a strict diet. Two months later he returned for a check-up. He had followed the diet carefully and had shed a lot of weight. "I feel so young," he told the doctor, "that in

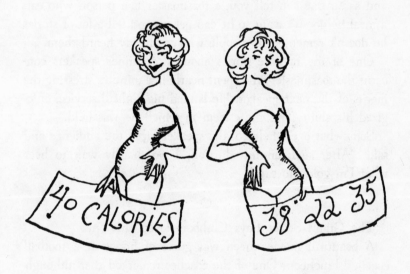

the elevator today I saw a girl bare her arm and I felt like biting it."

"You could have, you know," said the doctor. "It's only 40 calories."

☺

Jack Wasserman and my friends at the New York Philanthropic League chose this story:

A rabbi and a pompous woman who were attending a luncheon were conversing.

"One of my ancestors," boasted the woman, "signed the Declaration of Independence."

"Is that so?" asked the rabbi. "One of mine wrote the Ten Commandments."

☺

I am often called upon to act as toastmaster at luncheons; and as anyone can tell you, a toastmaster is a person who eats a meal he doesn't want so he can get up and tell a lot of stories he doesn't remember to people who've already heard them.

One of my favorite stories about after-dinner speakers concerns the toastmaster who spent nearly five minutes stressing the merits of the next speaker. He lauded his faithful service, eulogized his ability and the esteem in which he was held.

Somewhat overwhelmed, the speaker faced the audience and said, "After such an introduction, I can hardly wait to hear what I'm going to say."

☺

The Grand Street Boys Clubbers loved this one:

A beautiful movie queen was guest of honor at a football coaches' luncheon. One of the coaches remarked that although Hollywood was glamorous the life of a movie star was nowhere near as thought provoking as that of a football coach.

"I disagree with you," said the actress.

"How can you?" asked the coach.

"Because," she replied, "I have probably devised more defensive plays than the whole lot of you put together."

☺

A speaker who had bored his audience for almost a half hour said, "After partaking of such a meal I feel if I had eaten another bite I would be unable to continue speaking."

From the far end of the room came an order to the waiter, "Give him a sandwich."

☻

When toastmastering, George Jessel strives to introduce everybody on the dais to avert hurt feelings. Once, at a dinner for Eddie Cantor, Jessel introduced everybody but one man. He looked at the fellow for a few moments, realized he didn't know him, and then said, "That guy down at the end—frankly, I don't know who he is. But he must be somebody because we don't let any jerks sit at this table."

☻

A comic was invited to be toastmaster at a luncheon. At the end of the affair, the chairman of the entertainment committee came over and presented him with his check.

The comic who was doing exceptionally well in night clubs and on TV at the time said, "Why don't you give the money to some worthy cause."

"Would you mind," asked the chairman, "if we add it to our special fund?"

"Not at all," said the comic. "What is the special fund for?"

The chairman replied, "It's to enable us to get a better comedian next year."

☻

And before I pay my check, I'd like to say that I've come to an important conclusion. All waiters are cowards! I have yet to see one brave enough to lay a check face up on the table.

DO NOT DISTURB

A comedian is just like any other average American who stays up all night and sleeps 'til noon. I know this sounds glamorous to most people, especially those who have to get up in time to be at work by 9 A.M. However, it isn't as wonderful as it seems.

I don't know whether you'll believe it, but there are many comedians who never heard of oatmeal. I know one comic who never saw the morning sunlight until a few months ago when he played an engagement during the day season in Alaska.

Another thing that you have to remember is that a comic does a great deal of traveling in order to play night club dates all over the country. Consequently, on any given morning he can be sleeping in a hotel room anywhere from Hawaii to Alaska. This poses another problem. You never know who's in the next room. And you know what they say about hotel rooms. The walls are so thin when you try to sleep and so thick when you try to listen.

I remember one occasion when I was particularly tired after appearing at Chicago's Chez Paree. I went back to my hotel and instructed the desk clerk that I wasn't to be disturbed 'til noon.

After I closed my night light, I began to hear the fellow in the next room snoring loudly. I tried to ignore him but I found it impossible. "Sir," I screamed, "could you please stop snoring?" He didn't hear me. This went on all night. I kept pleading with him to stop snoring but it was to no avail. The next morning when I was leaving my room, I met him in the hallway. He eyed me suspiciously and took special notice of my bleary eyes. Then he said, "You know, fellow, you're a terrible guy to have a room next to. You talked in your sleep all night long!"

☺

Speaking about insomniac comics, one of my favorite stories, told to me by my Chicago friend, Ira Arkin, deals with the one whose doctor gave him a box of colored pills and told him, "Take one of these pills before you go to bed tonight. You'll not only sleep but you'll take a trip. You'll wake up in Paris." Next morning, the comic called the medico and said, "Doc, I slept. But no trip. I'm right here at home." "What color pill did you take?" the doctor asked. "Yellow." "Darn," said the physician. "You made a mistake. You took the round-trip pill!"

☺

Lou Wills, Jr. knew a funnyman who was even in worse shape. Lou met him on the street one day and the fellow looked awful. He had rings under his eyes. His shoulders drooped, and a list-less air marked his every movement. Even his voice sounded tired. He told Lou, "I couldn't sleep a wink last night. It's that rotten insomnia again." Lou nodded sympathetically. "I can appreciate how you feel, but why don't you try the old remedy of counting sheep at night?" Angrily, the guy replied, "Lou, you know darn well I'm a vegetarian!"

☺

Michel Rosenberg is another comic who likes to sleep late. However, he claims he hasn't had a good night's sleep in more than twenty-five years. I met him on Broadway once, and he looked completely fatigued. "What's the matter, Michel?" I asked. "Didn't you get any sleep last night?" "Yes, I slept," he answered, "but I dreamed that I didn't."

☺

And then there was the comic who stayed up all night and had daymares.

☺

When a comic sleeps late, and most of us do, the person who suffers most is his wife. She has to wait until her spouse arises before she can clean the bedroom and make breakfast. If she has something really important to do, like buying a new mink or playing mahjong, she may be held in the house 'til two or three in the afternoon because of a sleeping spouse. Recently, when Cindy Adams wanted to wake spouse Joey, she started screaming, "Brigitte Bardot! Brigitte Bardot!" Joey immediately leaped out of bed and raced into the kitchen. "Where is she?" he panted. "Oh, she's not here," Cindy pouted, "but I knew if I yelled 'breakfast! breakfast!' you would have never gotten out of bed."

☺

Sam Bramson, my representative at the William Morris office, heard a comic's wife tell him, "You need a self-starter to get you up in the morning." He replied. "Not when I have a crank like you to get me going."

☺

Milton Berle says he knows a great way to get comics out of bed. He's thinking of inventing an alarm clock that emits the

delicious odors of frying bacon and fragrant coffee. It's a novel idea, but is it kosher???

☺

Another weapon that comedians' wives use to get them out of bed is a common household possession which can be found in almost every home—KIDS.

One of my favorite stories concerns the young son of a comic who walked into his father's bedroom, woke him up, and asked for a drink of water. "Let your mother get it for you," growled the funnyman. The kid left the room but was back again in five minutes. Once again his father sent him on his way. This continued at regular intervals for the next half hour. Finally, the father could take no more. "If you come in here once more," he barked, "I'll get up and spank you." Undaunted, the lad returned five minutes later and announced, "Daddy, when you get up to spank me, will you bring me a drink of water?"

☻

Jerry Lewis' wife Patti had to go shopping recently and left her three oldest sons home with Jerry who was trying to get some sleep. About an hour after she left, the three lads woke Jerry up and told him, "We did all the dishes, Dad." "That's wonderful," yawned Jerry. "How did you manage?" "I," said the oldest, "washed them." "And I," said the next, "dried them." "And I," said the youngest, "picked up the pieces!"

☻

Morey Amsterdam was awakened from a pleasant snooze when his son Gregory, who had a cold at the time, was sniffling in the next room. "Haven't you got a handkerchief?" Morey asked. "Yes," replied Gregory, "but mother told me not to lend it to anyone."

☻

A comic who was trying to get some sleep after an exceedingly difficult night club date (no one laughed at his jokes) was awakened by his young son who asked, "What did you do at the Copa last night?" "Nothing!" screamed the annoyed father. After a thoughtful pause, the boy inquired, "Pop, how do you know when your act is over?"

☻

The precocious son of a comedian, who prefers to remain nameless, constantly woke his father up. "The next time you wake me," hollered the sleepy one, "I'll spank you. I'm getting tired of your juvenility." "Well," answered the youngster in one of his rare rebellious moods, "I'm getting fed up with your adultery!"

☻

A Jack Paar slumber was interrupted when his cute little daughter Randy tapped him on the shoulder and showed him an adorable pup which she had found in the street. "What kind of a dog is that?" questioned Jack. "It's a police dog," Randy announced proudly. "A police dog? He doesn't look like one," said Jack. "Oh I know it," was Randy's answer, "but you see, daddy, he's in the secret service!"

☻

When Phil Silvers' little daughter woke him up, he scolded, "Didn't you promise to be a good girl and that you wouldn't make any noise." "Yes, father." "And didn't I promise you a spanking if you weren't." "Yes, daddy, but since I've broken my promise, you don't have to keep yours."

☻

When the son of a very talented but extremely homely comic made enough noise to wake Rip Van Winkle, the funnyman arose to find the kid staring into the mirror. "Daddy, did God make you?" the boy asked. "Certainly, he makes everybody." "That means he made me too, right?" "Of course, what makes you ask?" The lad replied, "Because, it seems to me that he's doing better work lately!"

☻

COMIC (After his son woke him up): Now, Bobby, why don't you go play with your little friends?
BOBBY: I have only one little friend, and I hate him.

☻

When Jan Murray's son Warren was a little lad, he came into his father's bedroom crying pitifully. "Mama doesn't want to give me a dark breakfast." "Dark breakfast?" asked the confused Jan. "What's that?" "Well," explained Warren, "last night she gave me a light supper, and I didn't like it!"

☻

Desi Arnez was jolted out of a sound snooze by the blast of a pair of six-shooters. As he picked himself off the floor, he came face to face with a rough shootin' tootin' hero of the old West—his son.

"Wass a matter?" asked Desi. "Where'd you get that outfit?"

"Mommy got it for me for school. Teacher said we're learning to draw tomorrow!"

☻

The young son of a night club comic came rushing home with his report card, raced into his father's bedroom, and screamed, "I got my report card today." His father who was completely worn out was more interested in getting some sleep at that particular moment. "Well," he humored, "just tell me if you were promoted?"

"Better than that, Dad," beamed the lad, "I was held over for another term."

☻

And as any comic will tell you, a sound sleep is the sleep you're in when it's time to get up.

CALLING ALL CARDS

A major portion of my afternoons are spent on the phone, and anyone who thinks talk is cheap need only look at my phone bill. I think I spend more time on the phone than the average telephone operator. In fact, I could almost guarantee that if I stopped making calls, A. T. & T. would drop five points.

Wherever I am, there's always someone I can call or who calls me to tell the latest stories.

Whenever he's in town, my boy Danny Thomas calls and we exchange our latest funnies. Let's tune in on a recent Cohen-Thomas conversation.

DANNY: Did you hear about the conceited actor?

MYRON: No, why was he conceited?

DANNY: When his wife sued him for divorce, she named his mirror as corespondent.

☺

MYRON: What spoils quickly?
DANNY: A kid with overattentive grandparents.

☺

DANNY: What's the best way to make a peach cordial?
MYRON: Buy her a drink.

☺

MYRON: What's the best way to drive a baby buggy?
DANNY: Tickle its feet.

☺

DANNY: What's the best way to prevent yourself from rushing through a meal?
MYRON: Eat in a restaurant where the service is slow.

☺

Then we switch to the "longies."
DANNY: Hear any good gangster stories lately?
MYRON: Sure, let me tell you one.

A former office boy with a local stock exchange firm was brought to trial by his ex-employer on the charge of stealing $1,000 in postage stamps. He retained a clever young lawyer who made a brilliant defense plea, and he was exonerated. After the trial, he rushed over to the lawyer, shook his hand, and said, "You were great. How can I ever repay you?"

"Just pay my fee, that's all," replied the lawyer. "It's $1,000. But there's no rush if you're a little pressed."

"Well," the office boy suggested, "I can't pay you in cash right now, but will you accept stamps?"

☺

DANNY: Now I've got one for you.

A hold-up guy became slightly confused when he shoved a note at a bank teller which read: "I've got you covered, hand over all the dough in the cage," and the teller handed him a note back—"Kindly go to the next window. I'm on my lunch hour."

☺

MYRON: Now I'll toss you an animal story.

A movie producer tossed an old can of film into a lot. A goat who was passing by found it and ate it. While he was eating, another goat passed by and asked, "How does it taste?" The feasting goat replied, "I liked the book much better."

☺

DANNY: How about this one?

A tomcat and a tabby were courting on the back fence when the tomcat leaned over to her and said, "I'd die for you, you beautiful thing."

The tabby gazed at him longingly and said, "How many times?"

☺

MYRON: Let's go to psychiatrists. Not real ones, just stories.

A psychiatrist told the brother of one of his patients, "It would be wise for you to stay away from your brother for a while. He's in the midst of terrible delusions of grandeur and thinks he's Brutus."

"But what does that have to do with me?" questioned the brother.

"Well," explained the headshrinker, "he thinks you're Julius Caesar!"

☺

DANNY: Here's a good "psychiatwist": An attractive woman visited a psychiatrist and told him, "I'm in love with a wonderful man, and he loves me too. Both our parents are agreeable to the marriage, and we feel certain that we will be happy."

"Well," asked the dome doctor, "what is your problem?"

"Oh, doctor," she moaned, "I just don't know what to tell my husband."

☺

Anyone who's acquainted with Ed Sullivan knows that, despite his "smile-less" reputation, he has a keen sense of humor and often breaks up when he hears a funny story.

Ed, who recently wrote a book about Christmas, laughed when I called and told him the one about the unemployed actor who applied for a Santa Claus job at a large midtown department store. The guy who interviewed him asked, "Have you any experience?"

"Yes," replied the actor. "I worked two winters in the biggest department store in Brooklyn, and once I worked in the Bronx."

"That would be fine for an off-Broadway store," the interviewer said, "but we can only use people with Broadway experience!"

☺

Leonard Lyons, of the New York *Post*, prefers psychiatrist stories so I called and told him this one.

A disheveled man stumbled into a psychiatrist's office, tore open a cigaret, and stuffed his nose with tobacco.

"I can see that you need me," the headshrinker told him. "How can I help?"

"Got a light?" the man asked.

☺

He countered by telling me the one about the psychiatrist who was discussing one of his cases with a colleague.

"This fellow," the dome doctor said, "was under the delusion that a huge fortune was awaiting him. He claimed he would receive two letters which would give him title to two of the biggest oil wells in Texas."

"Well, what happened?" asked the other psychiatrist.

"It was a difficult case, and I worked hard on it. And just when I had the man cured, the two letters arrived."

☺

Earl Wilson, whose "Earl's Pearls" are famous throughout the country likes "quickies" so I phoned to give him this one:

When Alaska became a state, the geographic center of the U.S. shifted from Kansas to South Dakota. Texas, however, remained self-centered.

Then he told me one:

Since Alaska became a state, the Eskimo population is rapidly becoming Americanized. In fact, some of them have even cut holes in the top of their igloos so they can stand up when they hear "The Star Spangled Banner."

George Jessel, America's Toastmaster General who's also the original "Man Who Came to Dinner," probably knows more stories than any man alive. When I get on the phone with Georgie it usually develops into a real "talk-a-thon."

He'll start off with one like this:

Two kids were talking about girls.

"Aw," said one, "Girls are a dime a dozen."

"Gee," sighed his pal, "and all this time I've been buying jelly beans."

☺

And then I'll come back with a similar one.

A little girl went to the zoo with her father. When she looked into the lion's cage she asked, "What would happen, Daddy, if the lion got loose?"

"Don't worry." smiled her father. "I would protect you."

The girl thought for a few moments and then asked, "But, Daddy, just in case the lion eats you up, what bus do I take home?"

☺

Then he told the one about the magician who was trying to sell his act to agent Johnny Pransky.

"I've got the greatest act in the world," he said. "I pull out 300 lighted cigars from nowhere, puff on each one of them, and then swallow the entire 300."

The amazed agent gasped, "You swallow 300 lighted cigars? How do you manage that?"

"It's simple," replied the magician. "I've got connections in Cuba and get 'em wholesale."

☺

I came back with the tale of the parking lot owner who called all his attendants into his office and told them. "We haven't had a single complaint about a dented fender all week. How can we make any money leaving that much space?"

☺

Marty Burden, Earl Wilson's strong right arm who also writes the New York *Post's* "Dining Out" column, chuckled when I called and reported on a recent trip I had made to California. "I went into a grove and picked some oranges. Then I went to Santa Anita and picked some lemons."

☺

Then he related the yarn about the husband who asked his wife why they never had any money.

"It's the neighbors dear," she replied. "They always do something we can't afford."

☺

The late Danton Walker, who covered Broadway for the New York *Daily News*, once called me and told about the slightly inebriated Shakespearean actor who, upon arriving home, forgot which apartment on the second floor he lived in. Standing in front of the one he thought was his, he questioned, "2B or not 2B?"

☺

Hy Gardner, the New York *Herald Tribune* columnist, who's making it big with those clever and informative interviews on his TV show, applauded when I called to tell him about the Texas cop who spotted a new Cadillac on the sidewalk in front of a large Dallas oil company.

He walked over to the fellow inside and ordered, "Let me

see your license. You know you can't park here."

"Who's parking?" replied the guy in the car. "I'm picketing."

☻

Then I told him the one about the New Yorker who lunched in a Houston restaurant and then discovered he only had one $1,000 dollar bill. A little embarrassed at its size, he figured it might be difficult for the cashier to cash it. But having no other recourse, he handed it to her. Not blinking an eyelash, she put it in the till.

"I knew you wouldn't have any trouble with that here," he smiled.

The cashier who was counting out his change looked up at him and asked, "With what?"

☻

I called Frank Farrell, the New York *World-Telegram* & *Sun* columnist, and told him about the actor who was explaining his act to an agent.

"My act is different," he claimed. "I can fly." Then, he took off, circled the room a couple of times, and made a perfect landing.

"So you can imitate birds," sneered the agent. "And what else can you do?"

☻

Speaking about agents, I like the story about the male half of a new dance team who walked into Charlie Rapp's office and told him, "Our act is sensational. At the finish, I take my partner by the hair and whirl her around for exactly thirty spins. Then I wind up the whole thing by heaving her through an open window."

Charlie paled. "You mean you heave her through an open

74

window. Do you do that at every performance?"

The dancer shrugged. "Nobody's perfect," he admitted. "Sometimes I miss!"

☺

And while we're on the subject of missing, I'm reminded of the banker who thought his daughter missed the boat when she married his son-in-law. One day, he met another banker on the street, and the fellow asked, "Is it true that your daughter got married?"

"That's right," replied the father sadly. "I spent $15,000 on her education, and she married a fellow who earns only $3,000 a year."

"So what are you complaining about?" observed his friend. "You're still getting 20 per cent on your money!"

☺

I called Walter Winchell, of the New York *Daily Mirror,* and he told me about the two beatniks who met on the street.

"Hello," said one. "How're you getting along?"

"Not bad," said the other. "I'm managing to keep alive."

The first beat eyed his friend for a moment and then asked, "What's your motive?"

☺

Then I told him the tale of the beatnik wife who told a surprise guest, "Next time phone before you come so I can have a chance to mess up the house."

☺

As well as being a top columnist for the New York *Mirror,* Harry Hershfield is one of the deans of storytelling. When we

75

get on the phone together, the stories really fly.

Once I called and told him about the producer who was dissatisfied with his head writer's latest effort.

"I want you to rewrite it and put more conflict into it," he said.

"Conflict?" asked the surprised writer.

"Yes," said the producer. "Let me explain the meaning of 'conflict' to you. One man wants to be a boxer, and the other wants to be a violinist, and they're Siamese twins. That's conflict!"

☻

Then he fired this one at me.

A movie script writer who had been plagued all his life by producers who screamed of "too many comedies," "too many mystery films," "too many love stories," and "too many others," finally wrote a story about a talking dog.

"This dog," he told a producer, "is the most talented animal who ever lived. He can talk in twenty-three languages, pitch with both hands, run a mile in one minute, and sing like Frank Sinatra."

"Wonderful," screamed the producer. "We'll make a fortune. This dog sounds sensational. What kind of a hound is he?"

"Boxer," said the writer.

"No good," said the producer derisively. "We've had too many fight pictures."

☻

Bob Sylvester, who writes those witty columns for the New York *Daily News*, called and told me about the kid who brought a dozen cats into his house.

"Why did you bring them in here?" howled his mother.

"Because I heard Daddy say he smelled a rat!"

☺

Dorothy Kilgallen, the *Journal-American* columnist, laughed when I called and told her about the law professor who was lecturing to a group of students.

"When you're fighting a case," he said, "if you have the facts on your side, hammer them into the jury. And if you have the law on your side, hammer it into the judge."

A student asked, "But what if you have neither the facts nor the law?"

"Then," answered the professor, "hammer the table!"

☺

Lee Mortimer, a top columnist for the New York *Mirror*, buzzed me and related the anecdote about the hypochondriac who visited a doctor to have his blood tested. The doctor glanced at the test results and smiled.

"You have nothing to worry about. Your blood is fine."

"Good," said the hypochondriac. "Now give it back to me so I can go home."

☺

Louis Sobol, who writes for the New York *Journal-American*, enjoyed the tale about the fellow who visited a fortuneteller and then told his fiancée, "He told me that I'm going to marry a blonde in a month."

She replied, "That's all right. I can become a blonde in a month."

☺

Nick Kenny, the poet, who writes a TV column for the New York *Mirror* in his spare time, called and told of the photographer who quit his job at a Hollywood studio because he claimed there were so many "yes men" around that he could never get a good negative.

☺

This made me think of the tale about the Hollywood star who started divorce proceedings three weeks before her wedding and of her sister who saved a piece of her wedding cake for her divorce lawyer.

☺

Speaking about actresses, I'm reminded of the one who had her own ideas about production props.

"I insist upon real liquor in a drinking scene," she told her producer.

"All right," he agreed, "if you let me use real poison in the murder scene."

☺

Equally "kookie" was the glamorous movie queen who was taking the required blood test before her first marriage. When the doctor asked if she knew what type she was, she replied, "I'm the sultry type!"

☺

Boots McKenna tells a story about an extremely socially conscious film actress who aspired to be a member of an ultraswank Beverly Hills country club. By exerting influence, she got a friend to submit her name to the club's screening committee. Two days later the committee voted, and she was turned down. When the news was broken to her, she asked, "Were there many blackballs against me?"

"Well, I'll tell you, Betty," her friend said. "Do you know what a bowl of caviar looks like?"

☺

And while we're telling stories about Hollywood, one of my favorites deals with the high-salaried script writer who confessed to a friend, "I keep getting richer and richer but somehow I have the feeling that my work isn't up to my old standard."

"Nonsense," soothed his friend. "You write as well as ever. Your taste is improving, that's all!"

☺

Bob Williams, the New York *Post* TV columnist, appreciated it when I called and told him about the coed who sent her mother a letter.

Dear Mom:

Please send me $50 for a new dress as soon as possible.

I've had eight dates with Alfred and I've worn every dress I brought with me.

Her mother replied by return mail.

Dear Daughter:

Be economical. Get another boy friend and start all over again.

☻

My stockbroker, Adolphus Roggenburg of Newburger, Loeb & Co., called and told me that Bell & Howell had just announced a split.

"Oh, what a shame," I said. "They've been together so long!"

☻

My brother Phil, who is a partner and sales manager for Forge Mills and is one of the funniest guys in the Garment Center (it runs in the family) is always on the phone with me. (I hope his partners don't read this.) Since he's always in contact with salesmen, he'll start off with something along these lines:

Two salesmen were discussing the number of women who had taken over key positions in their organization.

"We don't have to worry," said one.

"Why not?" questioned the other.

"Because," said the first, "a woman salesman wouldn't know what to talk about. Who ever heard of a travelling saleswoman joke?"

☻

I came back with this one:

A Martian landed in a Madison Avenue ad agency and tapped a secretary on the shoulder.

"Take me to your leader," he said.

"I'm sorry, you'll have to wait," the secretary replied. "He's at the doctor's getting his ulcer checked."

☻

80

Then he told of the grocer who was praising a new minister.

"Have you heard the minister preach?" the grocer was asked. He said he hadn't.

"Then how do you know he's good?" someone asked.

"Because," the grocer answered, "his members have begun to pay their bills."

☺

I followed with the story of the Japanese flight commander who was briefing his kamikaze pilots.

"Fliers of Japan," he declared, "you are going on a sacred mission. I want you to shoot down all the American planes in the sky. I want you to shoot down all the American pilots, all the gunners, all the radiomen.

"Then I want you to take your planes and fly them directly into all the American ships. Sink the aircraft carriers, sink the cruisers, sink the battleships. Blow yourself into a thousand pieces for the glory of Japan and the Emperor."

Then he took a breath and said, "Any questions?"

One Japanese pilot shook his head in disbelief. "Commander," he asked, "you out of your gosh darn crazy mind?"

☺

Marie Torre, the New York *Herald Tribune* TV critic, likes gags with a video flavor.

A mother was telling her friend about her daughter's impending marriage.

"Mary and her future husband," she said, "are a very ambitious couple and refused to accept any help from us. They're starting out with just what they have to have—bed, stove, and television set."

☺

And speaking about TV, how about the TV producer who told his right hand man, "I wasn't always so prosperous. I was born poor and had to make my first pile playing a horse."

"At the races?" asked the aide.

"No," replied the producer, "in vaudeville."

☺

Bugs Baer, the New York *Journal-American* quipster, called to tell of the woman who was walking across the street when a reckless driver sped by and narrowly missed her. Realizing that it had been a close call, he backed up to apologize. However, before he could say a word, the woman noticed a pair of baby shoes dangling from his rear-view mirror and said, "Young man! I believe you should put your shoes back on."

☺

I happened to pick up the extension one day when my wife was speaking to a friend. It seems Mrs. X could not keep a maid for any length of time.

"How long was your last maid with you?" my wife asked.

"She never was with us," her friend replied. "She was against us from the start."

☺

On another occasion I caught this one between my spouse and another friend.

FRIEND: We've figured out a way to keep Harry from being late to school.

MRS. C.: What is it?

FRIEND: We bought him a car.

MRS. C.: But how did that help?

FRIEND: Now he's got to get there early to find a parking space!

☺

I phoned Atra Baer (Bugs's daughter) who writes TV columns for the New York *Journal-American* and told her this one:

Two Indians on an Oklahoma reservation were watching a husband and wife in the midst of a terrible argument.

"What do you suppose the trouble is?" asked one.

"The way I figure it," replied the other, "when they smoked the peace pipe, neither one inhaled!"

☺

Which reminds me. Did you hear about the adult western movie in which the Indians sat around the campfire, smoked their peace pipes, and complained about the high price of tobacco? Or the western so adult that the medicine man was a graduate of Johns Hopkins?

☺

And how about the one concerning the two TV stars who met at the door of a psychiatrist's office?

"Are you coming or going?" asked one.

The other replied, "If I knew, I wouldn't be here."

☺

Ben Rosenberg, the New York *Post* amusement editor, was amused when I called and told him of the teacher who was reading to her class when she came across the word *unaware*.

"Does anyone know the meaning of the word?" she asked.

"Unaware," a kid in the back yelled out, "is what you put

on first and take off last!"

☻

And before I put my phone back on the hook, I want you to remember this: a telephone is a device which makes it easy to distinguish voices and hard to extinguish them.

THE COCKTAIL HOUR

While touring the country, I've met some of the most unusual drunks. One disciple of the bottle told me he continually kept drinking because he wanted to avoid hangovers. Another said he drank to forget, but the only thing he ever forgot was when to stop. A third said he came from an alcoholic family and was fourteen before he learned toast was also a piece of bread.

I was passing a bar on Broadway one night when I saw an alcoholic actor I knew seated on a stool stripped to the waist. A sun lamp was focused on him. I walked in and asked, "George, are you all right?"

"I'm fine thanks, Myron," said my tipsy friend. "It's just that I told my wife I was spending the week in Florida."

☺

It had been a big night in the saloon down in Tombstone Gulch. When Cactus Sam opened his bleary eyes the next morning in his shack, he was startled to see a huge, hideous ape perched on the foot of his bunk, grinning at him. Slowly reaching for his gun, Sam took careful, if wavering aim.

"If you're a real ape," he uttered grimly, "you're in a damn bad fix. But if you ain't, I am!"

☺

"A lot of men," says Dick Shawn, "would live on liquid diets if it weren't for pretzels."

☺

An alcoholic meandered into the bar and placed one foot on the rail with difficulty. "Gimme a shot of Scotch and a shot of water," he ordered.

Surprised, the bartender, nevertheless, did as he was bid. He set up a jigger of Scotch and a jigger of water. And he watched in fascination as the lush pulled a worm from his vest pocket. With great deliberation, he dropped the worm into the jigger of water where it swam around with much nonchalance. Then, carefully, he took the worm out of the water and dropped it into the Scotch. Instantly, the worm began to writhe and wriggle. In another moment, it curled up and was dead.

"Shee," roared the drunk in triumph. "That proves it. Keep on drinking and you'll never have worms."

☺

BILL: So you've quit drinking?
PHIL: Yes, I did it for the wife and kidneys.

☺

And then there was the guy who drank so much you could hear the pretzels splash as he kept eating them.

☺

The Kentucky Colonel was asked why he always closed his eyes when he drank a mint julep. "Waal," he explained, "the sight of good lickah always makes my mouth water, and I don't aim to have my drink diluted."

☺

A man who celebrated a little too much one night woke up in the hospital the next day and saw his friend sitting beside his bed.

"What happened?" he asked.

"Well," began his friend, "last night you had quite a load on and went to a window, stepped over the sill, and announced you were going to fly around town."

"And you didn't try to stop me?" screamed the injured man.

"No, at the time I really thought you could do it."

☺

The long suffering wife was about to berate her husband for staggering home at 5 A.M. "Before you begin," he warned her, "I want you to know I was sitting up with a sick friend."

"A likely story," said his spouse. "What was his name?"

The husband gave this problem deep thought, then announced triumphantly, "He was so sick he couldn't tell me."

☺

A couple of happy celebrants were weaving their way home one night.

"Shay," said one, "won't your wife hit the ceiling when you

walk in tonight?"

"She probably will," said the other. "She's a lousy shot!"

☺

Herb Rau of the Miami *News* applauded when I told him this one:

An alcoholic who wasn't feeling well went to see his doctor. After a thorough examination, the physician reported to his patient that he had too much water in his body. "But I've never drunk a drop of water in all my life, Doctor." He paused for a second, then sadly concluded, "Must have been the ice."

☺

"I'm drinking to forget."

"In that case, please pay in advance."

☺

His wife was waiting when he arrived home.

"Oh, Allen!" she screamed, "you've done it this time. Besides being a mess and a drunken bum, you've also lost me the best maid I ever had. And you know how hard it is to get a good maid."

"What'd I have to do with the maid leaving?" asked the tipsy one.

"You insulted her over the phone, that's what you did. She said she had never heard such vile, insulting language in her life, and she packed up and left."

"Gee, honey, I'm sorry," comforted the drunk. "I thought it was *you* I was talking to."

☺

A fellow came into a bar and ordered a martini. Before drinking it, he removed the olive and carefully put it into a small glass jar. Then he ordered another martini and did the same thing. After an hour, when he was full of martinis and the jar was full of olives, he staggered out.

"Well," said a customer, "I never saw anything as peculiar as that."

"What's so peculiar about it?" the bartender said. "His wife sent him out for a jar of olives."

☺

"Nobody likes to be beaten to the punch," says Ed Wynn. "Especially if it's been spiked."

☺

Sign on a bar: DO A GOOD DEED AND HAVE A DOUBLE. IT'LL KEEP US AND ALCOHOLICS ANONYMOUS IN BUSINESS.

☺

And then there was the lush who stared into a mirror, noticed his bloodshot eyes, and said, "I'll never go into a bar again. Those television sets are ruining my eyes!"

☺

A drunken intellectual was arrested for speeding and brought before a judge. "Have you anything to say before you're sentenced?" asked the man on the bench.

"No," said the drunk. "I only converse with people of the arts—Hemingway, Picasso, Faulkner . . ."

"That's enough," interrupted the judge. "Ten days. And officer, take down the list of names he mentioned and round them up. I think they may be as bad as he is."

☺

A bartender who had no money offered a lawyer several

bottles of liquor if he would handle his case. The lawyer counted the bottles, shook his head, and told the bartender, "Only eight bottles of Scotch. I can't make a case out of that."

☺

PROFESSOR: How do you explain that barrel of beer I found in your room?

FRESHMAN: Doctor's orders, sir. He said that drinking beer would restore my health.

PROFESSOR: And did it?

FRESHMAN: Yes, sir, when I bought that barrel I could hardly move it, and now I can push it all around the room.

☺

Sid Fields of the New York *Mirror* likes this one:

A comic who always seemed to be drunk had a manager who tried to break him of the habit. After endless hours of telling the funnyman how John Barleycorn would ruin his career, the manager believed he had finally reached him. However, a few nights later the actor failed to show up for a night club date. The manager waited around until thirty seconds before curtain time and then sailed out to do the bars for his comic. He found him draped across a bar in a happy alcoholic haze.

"Good God," the manager cried, "you're on!"

The comic downed another drink. "I am?" he asked. "Great. How'm I doing?"

☺

And Hinson Styles, also of the New York *Mirror*, likes this one:

The judge looked sternly down at the defendant. "Young man." he said, "it's alcohol, and alcohol alone, that's responsible for your present sorry state!"

"I'm sure glad to hear you say that, Your Honor," the man replied with a sigh of relief. "Everyone else says it's all my fault."

☺

And then there was the drunk who started to write a drinking song but never got past the first two bars.

☺

A tall muscular man walked into a bar, looked the crowd over, and said, "I'm the toughest guy in town; yes, the fightenest man in this state; in fact, I'm the toughest guy in the world."

With that a little fellow who was standing at the other end of the bar walked over and socked him right on the chin. The muscular man fell back, banged his head against a stool, and dropped to the floor unconscious. When he came to, he dopily glanced at the fellow who had hit him and asked, "Who are you?"

"Me," came the reply. "I'm the guy you thought you were when you came in here."

☺

"Why is it," says Lou Holtz, "that drunks never spill drinks on other drunks?"

☺

A lion escaped from his cage and a posse was hastily formed to track him down. Before the search began the men stopped in a saloon where they all ordered drinks. All, that is, except one.

"Oh, come on," he was urged. "Have a drink with us."

"Not me," said the guy in a shaky voice. "Whiskey gives me too much courage."

☺

"A lot of wives whose husbands come home half shot," says comic Gene Baylos, "feel like finishing the job."

☺

Returning home late from a meeting, the minister noticed one of his congregation staggering down the street.

"Let me help you to your door," he said, guiding the inebriated member of his flock gently home.

Arriving at his house, the drunk pleaded with the minister to accompany him inside. "Please Rev'ren," he pleaded, "just for a minute. I want the missus to see who I've been out with tonight."

☺

The owner of a bar told his bouncer, "Throw that drunk out

—but don't antagonize him!"

☺

"Before we got married, my wife said to me, 'Lips that touch liquor shall never touch mine,' and I agreed with her."

"And you stuck to it?"

"Certainly, I have. I haven't kissed her for forty years!"

☺

Two drunks wandered into a zoo and stopped in front of a lion's cage. They stood watching the animal a few minutes and suddenly it let out a roar. "C'mon, let's go," said one.

"Go ahead if you want to," said the other. "I'm gonna stay for the movie."

☺

Jack Kahner told me the one about a drunk who staggered home and made his way into the house. As he groped about, he staggered into the shower and turned on the water. It made so much noise that it awakened his wife.

She was so infuriated to see her spouse making such a mess of the bathroom that she proceeded to give him a stern lecture concerning his past, present, and future.

"You're absolutely right, honey," the inebriate agreed amiably. "I'm everything you say. But please let me in. It's raining out here."

☺

"No man should drive a car while intoxicated," says Red Skelton.

"It's hard enough to get the pedestrian you're after while you're sober."

☺

A commuter approached the lost-and-found department of the Long Island Railroad. "I left a bottle of gin on the train last night," he said. "I thought it might possibly have been turned in."

"No, it wasn't," the clerk told him, "but the man who found it was."

☺

"Are you drinking again? Doesn't your health mean anything to you?"

"Yes, it means something to drink to."

☺

Two inebriated gentlemen, says Allan Bregman, stood at the bar near closing time.

"I've got an idea," said one. "Lesh have one more drink and then go find shum girls."

"Naw," replied the other. "I've got more than I can handle at home."

"Great," replied the idea man. "Then lesh have one more drink and go up to your place."

☺

"Poor man," a kindly old lady told a lush. "Is whisky your only comfort?"

"No ma'am," he replied. "I can drink beer when I have to."

☺

"Frank," stormed the corporal, "if you'd only stay sober and obey regulations you could become a corporal like me. Isn't that worth staying sober for?"

"Heck, no!" exclaimed Frank. "When I'm drunk, I'm a general."

☺

94

A workman was fixing one of those big tower clocks when a drunk looked up from the sidewalk and said, "Man, is that guy nearsighted!"

☺

The man went into a bar and ordered a glass of beer. He drank half of it and threw the rest at the bartender. Then he apologized profusely. "It's a nervous compulsion I have. I'm terribly embarrassed by it," he explained.

"You'd better consult a psychiatrist," the bartender said.

Several months later the man came back to the bar and did the same thing again. The bartender was naturally indignant.

"I thought you were going to see a psychiatrist," he said.

"I've been seeing one," said the man.

"It certainly hasn't done you much good."

"Oh, yes it has," the man replied. "I'm not embarrassed about it any more."

☺

Did you hear about the termite that walked into a tavern and asked, "Where is the bar tender?"

☺

"How did you spend the weekend?"

"Fishing through the ice."

"Fishing through the ice? For what?"

"Olives."

☺

A fellow was speeding down a highway when his car swerved sharply, crashed into a fence, and then rolled over several times. A farmer who was watching ran over just in time to see the driver crawl out of the wreckage. "Are you drunk?" he asked.

"You darn fool!" shouted the autoist. "Of course I'm drunk! What do you think I am—a stunt driver?"

☺

Sign over a bar: OUR MARTINIS ARE SO DRY THEY'RE DUSTY!

☺

FIRST MAN: What would you do if you had all the money you spent on beer?

SECOND MAN: I'd buy some more beer.

☺

A man bumped into an acquaintance in a bar and remarked, "I thought you'd given up drinking. What's the matter, no self-control?"

"Sure, I've got plenty of self-control. I'm just too strong to be a slave to it."

☺

Dean Martin claims his drinking goes back a long time. When he was in high school, he was voted most likely to dissolve.

☺

An airline passenger who had indulged rather freely before boarding the plane annoyed the pretty stewardess by demanding a martini. Finally, she brought him a plate with a lone olive resting in its center.

"What's that?" he wanted to know.

"That, sir," smiled the stewardess with her best smile, "is what you might call a *very* dry martini."

☺

Did you hear about the friendly alcoholic? He was always shaking hands—even when no one else was around.

And then there was the Toronto drunk who was found muttering, "It can't be done! It can't be done!" as he looked up at a big sign which read: DRINK CANADA DRY.

A husband, who came home one night in an extremely inebriated state, handed his wife twenty dollars.

"Twenty dollars," she screamed. "Where's the rest of your pay check?"

"I bought something for the house," he said.

"Oh," she replied, almost apologetically. "What?"

"A round of drinks."

A bouncer threw a noisy customer out of a bar four times in a row, and each time the unwanted imbiber would stagger back for more. At last a customer, who had watched with interest, tapped the bouncer on the shoulder.

"Know why that lush keeps coming back in?" he said.

The bouncer shook his head.

"You're putting too much backspin on him."

The much-married Hollywood actor was in a bar one night when he spotted a beautiful woman sitting by herself in the corner. He sat down next to her, turned on the charm, and said, "Pardon me, may I buy you a drink?"

"You certainly may," she replied. "I happen to be your wife."

"Today's homes have all the modern conveniences," says Hollywood *Reporter* columnist Mike Connolly, "but there are still many people who prefer to live in bars and taverns."

☺

A fellow was awakened at 3 A.M. by a drunk who pounded insistently on the door. The sleepy man opened the bedroom window and shouted to the inebriate below.

"Go away, darn it. You're trying to get into the wrong house!"

"Oh, yeah?" answered the drunk, "an' how do you know that you're not looking out of the wrong window?"

☺

Two old college classmates met after many years in a bar. They hoisted a few together, and then one asked if the other noticed the time. "Holy smoke! Doesn't your wife raise the dickens when you stay out late like this?" he asked.

"No," his friend replied. "I'm not married."

"Not married!" exclaimed the first man. "Then why do you stay out late like this?"

☺

A man raced into a psychiatrist's office and pleaded, "Doc, you've got to help my brother. He thinks he's an olive."

"Why do you say that?" asked the head shrinker.

"Because," replied the distraught brother, "he keeps sticking his head in other people's martinis."

☺

Two drunks were babbling about cradle days as they leaned heavily against the bar.

"You know," said one, "when I was born, I only weighed a

pound and a half and thash a fact."

"You don't shay," said the other. "Did you live?"

"Did I live!" exclaimed the first. "Shay man, you ought to she me now!"

☺

A fellow was drinking a Tom Collins mixed with second-rate gin one day when a friend passed by.

"Don't you know," warned the friend anxiously, "that stuff's slow poison?"

"Oh, that's all right," said the drinking one. "I'm in no hurry."

☺

A drunk was brought before the judge for the umpteenth time.

"Sam Brown," said the magistrate with severity, "you are charged with habitual drunkenness; what have you to offer in excuse for your offense?"

"Habitual thirst, your Honor."

☺

The story is told about the two men seated at a bar who became drunk after downing more than a dozen drinks each. The bartender, noticing their state, decided to give them ginger ale instead of liquor the next time they ordered. When one of the pair took a sip of the ginger ale, he bent over to his companion and whispered, "Drink up quickly! The bartender made a mistake. He gave us champagne instead of rye."

☺

He staggered up the walk with a silly grin and a faltering

step. She saw him a block away. "You're drunk again!" she shouted. "Well, if I ain't, I spent ten dollars foolishly."

☺

Danny Thomas often tells of the elderly gentleman who strolled into a neighborhood bar. He ordered two Scotch on the rocks. He drank one, then the other.

He did this for about three weeks. Then one afternoon the bartender said, "Sir, if I may suggest—why don't you order one drink at a time instead of two simultaneously? This way, while you let one drink stand until you finish the other, the ice dilutes it."

The dignified gentleman nodded. "Well," he explained, "there's a story behind my ordering two Scotch on the rocks. For years I used to have lunch with my partner, and each of us would take a Scotch on the rocks. After a while we made a pact that in the event that either of us died, the other would order two Scotches and drink a silent toast to the one who wasn't there."

The bartender agreed it was a touching ritual. A month later, however, the gentleman ordered only one Scotch on the rocks.

His curiosity aroused, the bartender asked, "Sir, how come you stopped ordering two individual drinks? Has your friend returned from the hereafter?"

"Not at all," the gentleman replied. "I'm ordering only one drink because I'm on the wagon."

☺

A friend described an alcoholic companion. "He's the nicest guy on two feet, if he could only stay there."

☺

"The difference between a rich drunk and a poor one," observed Olsen and Johnson, "is that a rich one tells his problems to a psychiatrist, and a poor one tells his to a bartender."

Two identical twins decided to have some fun one night. They dressed exactly alike and seated themselves side by side in a bar, ordering the same drink. Soon, a drunk staggered in and stared at them. He kept rubbing his eyes until one of the twins burst out laughing.

"It's all right," he smiled. "You're really not seeing things. We're twins."

The drunk looked again, blinked, and asked, "All four of you?"

"Bill was held up on the way home last night."
"Yeah, that's the only way he could have got home."

My invaluable friend, Jimmy McWhan, of the Pennsylvania Railroad, added this to our last telephone conversation:

A little boy came home and smelled liquor on his mother's breath. "Why, Mother," he exclaimed, "you're wearing Daddy's perfume."

☺

At cocktail hour, a group of businessmen were downing their martinis before going home. One of them, talking loudly after his fourth drink, suddenly turned away from the bar and fell flat on his face.

"One thing about Jack," remarked the bartender, "he always knows when he's had enough."

☺

And then there was the incurable lush who was drunk more often than water.

☺

A man brought a large dog into a saloon and sat down on a stool. Immediately, the dog jumped over the bar and began to bark.

"What's he barking about?" asked the saloonkeeper nervously.

"He always mixes my martinis," said the dog's owner, "and he wants to know if I'll have it dry this time." He turned to the dog. "Dry," he said, pointing to his throat and gasping.

The dog ran along the bar, got the gin bottle and the dry vermouth, mixed them in a mixing glass with ice cubes, poured them into a martini glass, and started alternately to roll on the floor and twist into odd contortions.

"See that?" said the man. "He wants to know if I want an olive or a twist of lemon peel." "Twist of lemon," he indicated, wringing an imaginary peel.

The dog finished making the martini, grabbed the dollar bill from the bar, ran to the cash register, came back with the exact change, and dropped it on the bar.

"Say," said the saloonkeeper, "I could make a fortune with that dog. How much will you sell him for?"

"Oh, you wouldn't want him," said the owner. "He forgets to take out for taxes."

☺

Sign on a bar: YOUR WIFE CAN ONLY GET SO MAD. WHY NOT STAY A LITTLE LONGER?

☺

FIRST MAN: I have no sympathy for a man who gets drunk every night.

SECOND MAN: A man who gets drunk every night doesn't need sympathy.

☺

A skunk, a rabbit, a seagull, and a peacock were seated in a night club. They each waited for the other to order the drinks. No one spoke.

Eventually the rabbit said hesitantly, "Don't look at me, boys, I've no doe!"

The skunk shrugged his shoulders. "You can count me out, I haven't got a scent."

The seagull looked around moodily. "I pass, I've been on the rocks lately."

So the peacock spoke up and said, "Okay, boys, the cocktails are on me."

☺

Did you hear about the guy who graduated from bartender's

school with high honors? He was the highest member of the graduating class.

☻

A lush walked into a bar and told the bartender he wanted a martini, extra rare.

"You mean extra dry," corrected the bartender.

"I mean extra rare," insisted the lush. "I'm having it for my dinner."

☻

"Did you have a tough time breaking into show business?" an actor renowned for his drinking was asked.

"Tough time!" he screamed. "Why things were so bad that sometimes I had to live for days on nothing but food and water."

☻

A nurse asked the wife of one of her patients, "I can't get your husband to take his medicine. Have you any suggestions?"

"Yes," said the wife. "He'll drink anything with foam on it."

☻

"A bartender," says Eddie Cantor, "is merely a psychiatrist who works in an apron."

☻

The noted alcoholic was telling a friend about a party he had attended the night before.

"Was it a good party?" asked the friend.

"It must have been," replied the lush. "I can't remember leaving it!"

☻

Two men were standing in front of a bar.

"You're a henpecked little jerk," said the first.

The other replied, "You'd never say that if my wife were here."

☺

Sign over a bar: THERE'S NO AMUSEMENT TAX HERE.

WHAT'S SO FUNNY ABOUT A HANGOVER?

☺

A wife described her husband's eating habits, "His idea of a balanced diet is a highball in each hand."

☺

The owner of a bar was describing a frequent visitor. "Although he spends a good deal of his time in my bar, he's still one of my unsteadiest customers."

☺

A lush staggered up to a cop in Times Square. "Pardon me, officer," he said, "but where am I?"

"You're at Broadway and Forty-second Street," said the cop.

"To hell with details," yelled the drunk. "What town am I in?"

☺

A pupil, aged nine, was asked to spell *straight*. He spelled it correctly and then his teacher asked, "Now what does it mean?"

The boy replied, "Without whisky or soda."

☺

The barber had a reputation for heavy drinking, and on a particular Monday morning there was a decided odor of whiskey on his breath. Suddenly the razor slipped and cut a nick in the customer's face.

"Now, Sam, you see what comes from too much drinking," the customer admonished gently.

"Yes, sir," replied the barber as he wiped the blood from the blade. "Drinking sure does make the face tender."

☺

A mink walked into a bar and ordered a double martini and explained to the bartender, "I want to taste it before I become a coat and get it spilled on me."

☺

"How would you define alcohol?"

"It's an excellent liquid for preserving almost anything but secrets."

☺

A fellow was stopped on the street by a weeping drunk.

"You've got to help me, buddy," pleaded the inebriated one. "I left home early this morning, and I haven't been seen since."

☺

And before we leave this chapter just remember this: some of the stuff they serve in bars today not only hits the spot, but removes it too.

NO PLACE LIKE HOME

The fellow who said there's no place like home must have been a bachelor. If he were a married man, he could never make such a statement. Marriage is a give and take institution. The husband gives, and the wife takes.

I like the story of the wife who told her spouse, "Jim, you don't love me like you used to. In fact, sometimes I think you don't love me at all."

"Don't love you at all," growled Jim. "There you go again. Why, I love you more than life itself. Now shut up and let me read the paper."

☺

A lawyer's wife was complaining about the way their home was furnished. "We need new chairs, a dining-room set, and a new lamp," she told him.

"Don't worry, dear," he calmed. "Just be a little patient. One of my clients is suing her husband for divorce. He has lots of money, and as soon as I finish breaking up their home, we'll fix ours."

☻

A millionaire was being interviewed about his self-made fortune. "I never hesitate," he said, "to give full credit to my wife for her assistance."

"And just how did she help?" asked a reporter.

"Frankly," said the millionaire, "I was curious to see if there was any income she couldn't live beyond."

☻

A rejected suitor told his girl friend, "If I had all the qualities you want in a man, I'd propose to somebody else."

☻

"I dreamed last night that you gave me a hundred-dollar bill to buy some new dresses today. Surely, you wouldn't do anything to spoil such a beautiful dream, would you?"

"Of course not, darling. To show you that I'm as generous as you dreamed, you can keep the hundred-dollar bill I gave you."

☻

The shortest romance on record:
"Wilt thou?" And she wilted.

☻

An enterprising suburban housewife was all set to start her spring cleaning when her spouse came home in a state of consternation.

"Alice," he exclaimed, "there are eight guys outside with

vacuum cleaners, and they all claim they have an appointment for a demonstration!"

"That's right," his wife replied blandly. "Now you just direct them all to different rooms and then tell them to start demonstrating."

☺

"Hello there, Irving. You're looking better. How's that pain in the neck?"

"Oh, she's playing mahjong."

☺

Joe E. Lewis says the modern wife is expected to look like a girl, behave like a lady, think like a man, and work like a dog.

☺

A little girl, sitting in a chapel watching a wedding, suddenly exclaimed, "Mother, has the lady changed her mind?"

"What do you mean?" the mother asked.

"Why," replied the child, "she went up the aisle with one man and came back with another."

☺

"You can still find wives who spend two hours preparing their husbands' suppers," claims Peggy Cass. "Some of those cans are tricky things to open."

☺

Bob Marshall tells of the woman who visited a psychiatrist and complained that her husband thought he was a pigeon.

"Why don't you bring him to see me," suggested the head-shrinker.

"All right, I will," replied the woman. "Just as soon as I can lure him down from the statue he's perched on."

☺

"When I can't tell whether my wife is coming or going,"
says Mark Wachs, "I know she hasn't been shopping."

☺

The attorney for the plaintiff in the divorce case put his
client on the stand.

"Now, as I understand it," he said sympathetically, "every
night when you returned from work, instead of having your
wife alone and awaiting you, you found a different man hiding
in the closet?"

"Yes. That's right."

"And this of course, caused you untold anguish and unhap-
piness, did it not?"

"Why, sure!" came the hurt reply. "I never had any room to
hang my clothes."

☺

WIFE: Do you love me?
HUSBAND: Yes.
WIFE: How much do you love me?
HUSBAND: How much do you need?

☺

A guy was taking an auto trip with his wife. She looked at
the road map and told him, "Darling, we're going in the wrong
direction."

"What's the difference," he replied. "We're making great
time!"

☺

A young fellow, just back from his honeymoon, was being enriched in wisdom by questioning a long-married friend.

"Now, about finances," he said. "Do you provide your wife with a checking account, monthly allowance, or whatever amount she requests?"

"My boy," smiled the older man. "I provide all three."

☺

"Early in life, men prefer girls with good figures," says Jack Carter. "But later, they wish they had preferred those who were good at them."

☺

Wife, reading her husband's fortune on a weight card: " 'You are dynamic, a leader of men, and admired by women for your good looks and strength of character' . . . It's got your weight wrong, too!"

☺

After the court awarded the woman a large marital settlement, they met once more in the corridor.

"I suppose you always had my best interests at heart," the husband said with resignation.

"I certainly did," she replied.

"Then," he roared, "why the hell did you marry me?"

☺

FIRST MAN: My wife is very considerate.
SECOND MAN: Why, what'd she do?
FIRST MAN: She went to Florida so I wouldn't have to buy her a box of candy for Valentine's Day.

☺

"We couldn't help hearing you and your wife having a battle last night," Phil's neighbor told him the next morning. "How'd you make out?"

"Fine, fine," Phil answered heartily. "In fact, by the time it was over, she came crawling to me on her hands and knees."

The neighbor, who knew Phil's wife, looked doubtful.

"It's a fact," Phil continued. "And she said, 'come out from under that bed, you coward'!"

☺

"My dear, you're wearing your wedding ring on the wrong finger!"

"I know. I married the wrong man."

☺

Martha Raye can't understand why any woman would want her husband to run for president. "The minute you move into the White House," says Martha, "everyone on the block knows exactly what your husband does and how much he makes."

☺

"If you had to choose between marrying for love or money, Helen, which would you choose?" asked her friend.

"Love, I guess," replied Helen. "I always seem to do the wrong thing."

☺

HUSBAND: You'll drive me to my grave!
WIFE: What'd you expect to do, walk?

☺

A young woman went to a fortuneteller.

"Very soon," droned the mystic, "you will meet a tall, handsome man who will sweep you off your feet. He will shower you with gifts, take you to breathtaking night spots, and the two of you will drink a toast to your everlasting love."

"Has he any money?" she asked.

"He is president of a large concern and heir to a million dollars."

"Gee!" she stammered. "Can you tell me just one more thing?"

"What do you want to know?"

"How can I get rid of my husband?"

☺

And while we're dealing with fortuneteller stories, how about this one?

"You will marry a dark man," said the fortuneteller, "and for the first few years of your married life you will be very unhappy."

"And after that?"

"You'll get used to it."

☺

"Maybe clothes don't make a man," observes New York *Journal-American* columnist Bert Bacharach, "but they can break a husband."

☺

A rather pompous fellow, hosting at a dinner said, "I wonder how many really great men there are in this world."

Without blinking an eyelash, his wife retorted, "Darling, there's one less than you think."

☺

A Hollywood producer, who stressed realism in his films,

had a script calling for a fight between two men on the street.

Discussing the scene with his star, he said, "Bob, do you see that couple waiting for the bus? I want you to go over and start insulting the woman."

"But why?" asked the confused Bob.

"Because," said the producer, "you'll get her husband fighting mad, and he'll haul off and belt you. That'll give the scene realism."

Bob went up to the couple. "Good day, sir," he said. "Is this your wife?"

"That's right," was the answer.

"What a hag!" roared Bob, getting ready for the first punch. "Why most men would be ashamed to be seen with her!"

There was an ominous silence. Then the man turned to his wife.

"See," he demanded. "What have I been telling you all these years?"

☺

"A bachelor," says Alan King, "is a guy who doesn't have to worry about how much of his take-home pay reaches there."

☺

When asked what he did before he was married, a husband replied, "Anything I wanted to."

☺

INSURANCE ADJUSTER: Why didn't you report the robbery at once?

HOUSEWIFE: I didn't suspect I'd been robbed. When I came home and found all the dresser drawers open and things scattered all over the place, I thought my husband had been looking for a clean shirt.

☺

The woman, who was visiting her husband in the hospital, took the pretty young nurse aside and asked, "Tell me the truth. Is he making any progress?"

"Absolutely not," the nurse replied. "He's not my type."

Irv Kupcinet of the Chicago *Sun-Times* likes this story:

A wife visited a furrier and tried on a mink coat. After studying herself in the mirror, she told him, "I'll take it on one condition."

"What is it?" he asked.

"If my husband doesn't like it, will you promise to refuse to take it back?"

A wife told her spouse, "I was just as unreasonable when we were first married but you thought it was cute."

And Bentley Stegner, also of the Chicago *Sun-Times*, prefers this one:

An office worker came in one day, sporting an engagement ring. An older colleague, seeing the ring, wished the girl every happiness.

"But let me offer you some advice," said the older woman. "Don't give him his own way too much. Demand your rights. When I got married, I insisted that my husband give up smoking and drinking.

"And did he?" asked the engaged girl.

"I don't know," admitted the adviser. "I haven't seen him in twenty years."

☻

"Does your wife drive?" asked Sam, looking at his friend's car.

"No," was the reply. "It was like this when I bought it."

☻

A hillbilly found a mirror while walking through the woods. He looked into it and exclaimed, "Why it's a picture of my old Pa." He took it home and hid it in the attic. His wife suspected something, went to the attic, and found it. When she looked into it, she said, "So that's the old hag he's been running around with."

☻

Speaking about suspecting wives, I like this story.

"City Hall," said the switchboard operator, answering a call. There was no sound at the other end of the line.

"City Hall," the operator repeated. Still no reply.

Finally, after the third time, a rather nervous female voice said, "Is this really City Hall?"

"That's right, madam," said the operator. "With whom do

you wish to speak?"

There was an embarrassed silence. Then the female voice said softly, "I guess nobody. I just found this number in my husband's pocket."

☺

Mrs. Dale informed her better half that she was expecting a party of guests. He immediately rose and hid all the umbrellas.

"Why," she exclaimed, "are you afraid the guests will steal your umbrellas?"

"No, I'm afraid they'll recognize them."

☺

"Could I see the burglar who broke into our house last night?" asked a caller at the police station.

"Why do you want to see him?" asked the officer in charge.

"I'd like to ask him how he got in without waking my wife."

☺

Did you hear about the extremely lazy wife? The only exercise she gets is running up bills and jumping to conclusions.

☺

Mrs. Newlywed inveigled her husband into a shopping trip. Once she got him to the most expensive jeweler in New York, she wangled a solid gold brooch, a diamond ring, a diamond bracelet, and a pair of earrings.

"Well," the dazed, much poorer husband said when they were in the street again, "what do we do now?"

"Now," said the wife firmly and virtuously, "I'm going to save you some money. We'll take the subway home."

☺

A guy asked a recent groom, "Is your wife's cooking anything to write home about?" The groom replied, "Yes, it's got me writing home for some of Mother's recipes."

☺

When some wives start running up expenses, they leave their husbands breathless.

☺

Two matrons were talking at a class reunion.
"What kind of a husband do you have?" asked one.
"Well, let me put it this way," said the other. "If he mentions Rose in his sleep, he's definitely talking about flowers."

☺

Three commuters were discussing their wives while waiting for their trains.
"I've got a wife who meets my train every night, and we've been married ten years," bragged the first.
"Well, I've got a wife who's been doing the same thing every night, and we've been married twenty years," said the second.
"I can beat that," said the third. "I've got a wife who meets me every night and I'm not even married."

☺

"The reason some married couples don't get along," says Shelly Berman, "is that they have nothing in common to fight about."

☺

"Give one reason why so many wives are opposed to divorce."
"They don't like the idea of sharing their husband's money with a lawyer."

☺

WIFE: Doctor, my husband has some terrible mental affliction. Sometimes I talk to him for an hour and then discover he hasn't heard a single word.

DOCTOR: Madam, that's not a mental affliction. That's a gift.

☺

"Marvin, do you love me still?"
"Yes—better than any other way."

☺

A woman who was spending the winter in Miami mentioned to her friend how hard her husband worked. "Sidney," she said, "is the hardest working man in the Garment Center. He puts in sixteen hours a day and works like a horse."

"Why doesn't he take a vacation?" asked the friend.

The wife replied, "Since when does a horse take a vacation?"

☺

And then there was the guy who complained to his wife that his secretary didn't understand him.

☺

"My husband and I both like the same things," Mrs. Goldberg told a neighbor. "But it took him twelve years to learn."

☺

"For twenty years," a man told his friend, "my wife and I were ecstatically happy."

"Then what happened?" questioned the friend.

"We met."

☺

HUSBAND: I hate to admit it, dear, but I bought another

ten-thousand-dollar policy from the life insurance salesman.

WIFE: Oh I could kill you.

☺

The man gazed rapturously at the jewelry counter in a department store.

Then, he spoke to the clerk: "These diamonds are really beautiful, aren't they? I'd like to smother my wife in them."

"Oh, that would cost a lot of money, sir," the salesgirl told him. "There must be a cheaper way."

☺

One morning at breakfast a wife was cross and irritable.

"What's the trouble?" asked her husband.

At first, his wife refused to tell, but finally, she turned to him with tears in her eyes and sobbed, "If I ever dream again that you kissed another woman, I'll never speak to you as long as I live."

☺

A henpecked husband told his spouse, "If you want my opinion give it to me."

☺

And then there was the sentimental daughter of a Hollywood beauty who wanted to get married in her mother's wedding gown but she couldn't decide which one.

☺

A much-married Hollywood actor was confronted by a gay damsel.

"Don't you remember me?" she greeted him. "Five years

ago you asked me to marry you!"

"Really?" yawned the actor. "And did you?"

☺

"I didn't know your husband was artistic."

"He isn't—he's just untidy."

☺

A fellow asked his pal about his spouse, "Does your wife economize?" His pal replied, "Yes, we can do without practically everything I need."

☺

"All men make mistakes," says New York *Journal-American* columnist Frank Coniff, "but husbands just find out about them sooner."

☺

A general, a colonel, and a major were discussing matrimony. The general contended that marriage was sixty percent work and forty percent pleasure. The colonel felt it was seventy-five percent work and twenty-five percent pleasure. The major felt it was ninety percent work and ten percent pleasure. While they were arguing, a private entered the room and the general suggested, "Let him decide."

The private listened to all sides of the argument and then announced his opinion. "If you'll excuse my saying so, sirs, matrimony must be one hundred percent pleasure and no work at all."

"How did you come to that conclusion?" demanded the surprised officers.

"It's simple," replied the private. "If there were any work

in it at all, you gentlemen would have me doing it."

☺

Two men met in a bar and soon began discussing their wives.
"My wife is an angel," said one.

"You're lucky," replied the other. "Mine looks as though she'll
live for years."

☺

A young couple were exchanging ideas on marriage.
"I won't get married," said the boy, "until I find a girl like
the one grandpa married."
"They don't have a woman like that today," said the girl.
"No?" said her boy friend with relish. "He just married her
yesterday."

☺

FIRST MAN: Have you noticed how reluctant the young men
of today are to marry and settle down?

SECOND MAN: I've noticed many times.

FIRST MAN: They seem to fear marriage. Why, before I was married, I didn't know the meaning of fear.

☺

Hinson Styles, of the New York *Mirror,* observes that a lot of girls who seem ideal before marriage turn out to be an ordeal afterward.

☺

Harry Pavony, the accountant for the Myron Cohen Foundation, heard a new bride asked by a friend, "Does your husband expect you to obey him?" "Oh, no," she replied. "He's been married before."

☺

"Nothing gives a wife that delightfully surprised feeling," says *Variety* editor Abel Green, "like receiving the birthday gift she's been hinting about for months."

☺

"Betty, you poor girl," gushed the voice on the phone, "I just heard your husband is in the hospital. What's wrong with him?"

"It's his knee," Betty explained.

"Oh, he broke it?" asked her friend.

"No," was the crisp reply. "I found a strange woman on it."

☺

FRED: I heard you entertained your neighbors informally last evening.

SAL: Yes, the missus and I had a fight on our back porch.

☺

A henpecked husband was telling a friend about his spouse. "She's very strict," he said.

"Would you say she always gets her way around the house?" his companion asked.

"I'll say," the husband agreed. "Why, she even writes her diary a week ahead of time."

☺

"I'm getting mighty exhausted contesting my wife's will," admitted Herb to a confidant.

"I never knew she died," said the shocked friend.

"That's the trouble," sighed Herb. "She didn't."

☺

The hostess poured a cup of tea for a middle-aged man at her party and asked if he took sugar.

"No," said he.

"Yes," his wife corrected him. "You know I always put sugar in your tea.

"I know," replied her husband. "I used to remind you not to. Now, I just don't stir."

☺

"Hiding a secret from your wife," says Lou Walters, "is like trying to sneak daybreak past a rooster."

☺

A man was complaining about his new son-in-law. "He can't drink and he can't play cards."

"That's the kind of son-in-law to have," said a friend.

"Naw," said the man. "He can't play cards, and he plays. He can't drink, and he drinks."

☺

"When a man opens the door of his car for his wife," says Jules Podell of the Copa, "you can be sure that either the car or the wife is new."

The judge looked at the man who was seeking to obtain a divorce. "You claim false pretense?" he asked. "Misrepresentation? Isn't that a rather curious reason to want a divorce? You will have to explain more fully."

"Oh, I can do that, your Honor," said the man readily. "When I asked this woman to marry me, she said she was agreeable. She wasn't!"

SOLOMON'S 999TH WIFE: Sol, are you really and truly in love with me?

SOLOMON: My dear, you are one in a thousand.

A bride-to-be had just shown a friend the list of wedding guests.

"Isn't it strange," said the friend "that you've included only married couples?"

"Oh, that was Phil's idea," the bride-to-be replied. "He says that, if we invite only married people, the presents will be all clear profit."

"My wife had a funny dream last night," confided a man to his friend. "She dreamed she was married to a millionaire."

"You're lucky," sighed his pal. "My wife dreams that in the daytime."

"The man of the hour," says Leo Shull of show business, "is often the husband whose wife told him to wait a minute."

☺

"Didn't I hear the clock strike two as you came in last night?" the wife asked her mate at the breakfast table.

"Yes, dear," replied the husband from behind the morning paper. "It started to strike ten, but I stopped it to keep it from waking you up."

☺

Did you hear about the husband whose wife made a lasting impression on him? The doctors say the scar will never disappear.

☺

"Wives are like cars," says *Variety's* Joe Cohen. "If you take care of them, you don't have to get new ones all the time."

☺

A woman phoned the Legal Aid Society for some advice. "I want to know if I can get a divorce because of my husband's flat feet?" she asked.

"Hmmm," answered the lawyer cautiously. "I don't think so, unless you can prove his feet are in the wrong flat."

☺

"How did you get to know your wife before you married?"
"I didn't know her before I married."

☺

Two young wives were chatting. "My husband can't stand music concerts," said one. "The opening bars send him home."

"You're lucky," replied the other. "Mine is sent home by the closing bars."

☺

A wife stood in front of a mirror fixing her hat until her beloved took notice.

"That hat looks awful on you," he grumbled. "Take it off and return it for credit."

"I can't very well return it," she replied happily, "because it's the one I've been wearing for two years. But since you dislike it so, I'll buy a new one tomorrow."

☺

MRS. BROWN: It seems to me that common sense would prevent many divorces.

MR. BROWN: It seems to me that it would also prevent just as many marriages.

☺

"With all those modern household appliances," notes Danny Dayton, "a man is better off marrying a girl who's a mechanical genius than one who can cook."

☺

The young bride appeared before her dinner guests carrying a tray full of cocktails.

"I hope these martinis are all right," she said. "We ran out of olives, so I just poured a spoonful of olive oil into each glass."

☺

"It's the men from the loan company," the bride explained to her husband as the burly men clumped upstairs. "They've come for the piano."

"But, darling," her husband protested, "I gave you this month's installment."

"I know," the bride answered. "And I intend to pay them as soon as they get the piano downstairs. I've decided I prefer it down there."

☺

"Despite all its advances," says Garry Moore, "modern science has yet to find an easy way for the average housewife to get breakfast in bed."

☺

Wife to husband at breakfast:
"You and your suicide attempts.
Look at this gas bill!"

☺

The lady of the house summoned a TV serviceman to fix the set. Spreading out his tools, the repairman inquired, "What seems to be the trouble?"

"Well, for one thing," replied the woman. "All the programs are lousy."

☺

"So," said the wife, "you love me with all your heart. Would you die for me?"

"No," said her spouse. "Mine is an undying love."

☺

"Darling," said the Hollywood bride as her new husband carried her across the threshold of her new home. "This house looks so familiar. Are you sure we haven't been married before?"

☺

128

The story is told of the fellow who was extremely devoted to his mother. He had lived with her for forty-three years and wouldn't wed for fear of offending her. Then, at a party, he met Mary.

After a brief courtship, the couple eloped and kept the merger secret for a year. Mary finally insisted that the truth come out or she would leave for Reno.

The couple called on his mother, and he tried to break the news gently.

"Mother," he quivered, "I hope you will understand and give us your blessing. I want you to know Mary and I have been married for a year."

The old lady looked stern.

"Mother," trembled the groom, "What is it? Don't you approve?"

"A fine thing!" cried the mother. "You and Mary have been married for a year, and I'm still doing your shirts!"

☺

A spouse who came home from a stag party with a black eye was asked by his wife, "Can you describe the guy who hit you?"

He replied, "That's just what I was doing when he hit me."

☺

"George and I had a terrible argument last night and he left home," a wife sadly told her friend.

"Oh, don't let that bother you," soothed her friend. "After all, he's done that before."

"Yes, I know," sobbed the unhappy spouse, "but this time he's taken his bowling ball."

☺

And then there was the man who met his wife at a travel bureau. She was looking for a vacation, and he was the last resort.

☺

Two housewives were discussing their mates. One mentioned that her husband was so wonderful that he treated her like a queen.

"You think that's something?" bragged the other woman. "Let me tell you how good my husband is. He treats me just like I was his mistress."

☺

Did you hear about the Hollywood couple who won't get a divorce until their son passes his bar exams? They want to be his first case.

☺

"And how is your daughter, Mrs. Scalyer—the one who got married last year? Is the marriage working out well?"

"Oh, yes, everything's fine. Of course she can't stand her husband, but then, isn't there always something?"

☺

"Well," said the husband. "I'm hardly home from the office and you're asking me for more money."

"It's your own fault," snapped the wife. "You were half an hour late."

☺

A woman who was divorcing her husband told the judge, "Your Honor, he swears at me in his sleep."

"That's a lie, your Honor," shouted the husband. "I'm not asleep!"

☻

"A gentleman," according to Bob Hope, "is a fellow who, when his wife drops something, kicks it to where she can pick it up more easily."

☻

A woman went to a psychiatrist because her husband thought he was a mink. "Your fee won't be any problem," she explained, "because he sheds a lot."

☻

And before we leave this chapter, I'd like to give one little piece of advice to roving husbands: ABSENCE MAKES HER HEART GO WANDER.

131

CAUGHT IN THE SPORTS WHIRL

When I have a free afternoon and the weather is nice, I like to go out to the nearest golf course and play 18 holes. It has been said that the course of true golf never runs smooth. However, one would never guess this from listening to golfers. Golf has made more liars out of Americans than fishing. In fact, nowadays, it's more popular than fishing because a golfer has a major advantage over a fisherman; he doesn't have to show anything to prove it.

One of my favorite golf tales deals with the wife who entered a sporting goods department of a large store and told the salesman, "I'd like a low handicap, please."

"A low handicap?" the man repeated puzzled.

"Why, yes," she said, "for my husband's birthday. He's always wishing he had one."

POOR GOLFER: Well, how did you like my game?

CADDY: I suppose it's all right, but I still prefer golf.

☺

"You think so much about your old golf game that you don't even remember when we were married," complained the wife.

"Of course I do, honey," the husband reassured her. "That was the day I sank that forty-foot putt."

☺

"If golf is played for exercise," questions Morty Gunty, "how come the player who manages to get the least of it wins?"

☺

Frank Coniff of the New York *Journal-American* tells of two golfers who were just leaving the eighteenth green. "That sure was a great drive I made off the first tee!" boasted one for about the tenth time. "Yes, sir, a real beauty!"

"It certainly was," agreed his companion who had spent the entire afternoon hearing about that one drive. "It's too bad you can't have it stuffed."

☺

Sam Snead and Ted Williams were having a friendly argument over whether golf or baseball is the tougher game. Finally Snead drawled, "Well, there's one thing about golf. When you hit a foul ball, you gotta get out there and play it!"

☺

"My doctor tells me I can't play golf."

"So he's played with you, too."

☺

"How long have you been playing golf?" the old club member asked the stranger on the fourth tee.

"Oh, about three months," the stranger replied.

"Well, you certainly play a very good game."

"I ought to," the stranger sighed. "It took me four years to learn."

☺

Golfing businessmen have a special problem. If they shoot above par, they are neglecting their golf and if they shoot below par, they are neglecting their business.

☺

Then, there's the story about the man in the foursome who drove his ball grimly from the first tee. It rose into the air nicely, like a jet airliner taking off from the runway. Then it made a crazy heartbreaking turn and disappeared over the treetops into the woods along the fairway.

The man's partner had his back turned at the time and didn't see the awful slice.

"Well, Frank," he remarked cheerfully, "that one sure sounded good."

"Yes," said Frank. "But I'm not giving a concert."

☺

"The traps on this course are certainly annoying, aren't they?" babbled a talkative golfer to his partner just as the latter was about to make a tough approach shot.

"Yes," his companion answered. "Would you please shut yours?"

☺

"So you played golf with Jim yesterday," remarked a college girl to her sorority sister. "How does he use the woods?"

"I don't know, I'm sure," answered the friend primly. "We played golf all the time."

☺

Two friends had a date to play golf. The first one stepped to the tee, took a mighty swing and his drive was a hole in one.

The second friend stepped to the tee and said, "All rightee, now I'll take my practice swing, and then we'll start the game."

☺

The two golfers had reached the last green in the competition final and, as the excited onlookers stood in hushed silence, the first player shaped up to putt. Just as the putter blade was moving nicely toward the ball, a spectator sneezed violently. The unfortunate golfer was startled and struck the ball with a jerky and indeterminate jab. The ball hit the back of the cup, rose a good four inches into the air, and dropped into the hole.

When the applause died down, the second player advanced to his ball and just before he was about to stroke, he turned his head toward the fellow who had sneezed.

"I wonder," he said politely. "Could you possibly manage another sneeze?"

☺

"Why do you play golf?"
"To aggravate myself."

☺

Ann Marsters of Chicago's *American* tells of the golfer who was brought into the hospital suffering from sunstroke. The nurse began to read his temperature. "102-102-103."

"Hey, Doc," whispered the suffering sport. "What's par for this hospital?"

☺

Two male golfers were highly annoyed by a pair of females on the links in front of them. The women stopped to chat, picked flowers, admired the scenery, and generally made life miserable for the players following.

At one point, the two men stood on a tee for nearly twenty-five minutes while one of the women apparently looked for her ball a few yards down the fairway.

"Why don't you help your friend find her ball?" one of the indignant golfers finally shouted to the second woman who stood watching her companion search.

"Oh, she's got her ball," the woman replied sweetly. "She's looking for her club."

☺

"Nowadays," claims Joe E. Brown, "another place where men aren't safe from women drivers is a golf course."

☺

"This game is so much more fun than golf!" exclaimed an enthusiastic young lady during her first night of bowling. "You're not always losing the ball."

☺

A snooty woman came off the links, stuck her nose into the air, and announced, "I went around in 76."

To which a rival iced, "With Paul Revere, no doubt."

☺

I always thought it was an amazing coincidence that so many men lose their grandmothers the opening day of the baseball season. However, despite its high mortality rate, baseball is a wonderful sport. It has many devoted fans. In fact, some of them are such fanatics that they'll go to a ball game even when their TV sets aren't busted.

☺

One of the most popular baseball stories deals with the one-time great pitcher who retired from the game and applied for a job with a public relations firm. He was given a routine questionnaire to fill out, and one of the questions asked for his last job and his reason for leaving. To the first part he wrote: "Pitching baseballs," and to the second part: "Couldn't get the side out."

☺

Clark Kinnaird of King Features Syndicate applauded when I told him this one:

A woman raced into a psychiatrist's office and pleaded, "Doctor, you must help my husband. He finds it impossible to make decisions." "Nothing unusual about that," soothed the dome doctor. "Lots of people find it difficult to make decisions." "But doctor, you don't understand," screamed the woman, "my husband happens to be an umpire!"

☺

FIRST BASEBALL PLAYER: You didn't fare too well with the owner's daughter, did you?

SECOND BASEBALL PLAYER: Terrible—no hits, no runs, no heiress.

☺

The runner rounded second base and headed for third as the outfielder uncorked a tremendous peg from deep center. Ball and runner arrived at the hot corner in a cloud of dust.

"You're out!" roared the umpire.

"I'm not out!" roared the angry runner.

"You're not?" The ump was surprised. "Well, just take a look at tomorrow's paper."

☺

Robert Dana of the New York *World-Telegram* & *Sun* appreciated this one:

A manager whose team was hopelessly mired in last place received a call from his head scout.

"I've just seen the greatest pitcher in the country," the talent hunter enthused. "He pitched a perfect game; twenty-seven strike-outs in a row. No one could even hit a loud foul off him until there were two out in the ninth. I've got the pitcher here with me now. What should I do?"

Without a second's hesitation, the manager replied, "Sign the guy who got the foul. We need hitters."

☺

And then there was the outfielder who had such a weak arm, the only thing he threw out in twenty years was his old glove.

☺

ADVICE TO BASEBALL PLAYERS: If at first you don't succeed, try second base.

☺

The last inning was over and the center fielder, who had

muffed an easy fly, came trotting past the manager. "I've gotta get movin' if you don't mind," said the ballplayer. "I've got a plane to catch."

"Go ahead," snarled the manager. "And better luck with the plane."

☺

"It's easy to pick out the ballplayer who's gone Hollywood," says Groucho Marx. "He's the one who wears dark sunglasses—even after the game."

☺

Two rooters at a ball game were so engrossed in the contest that neither wanted to march back to the refreshment stand for hot dogs, and there wasn't a vendor in sight. They finally bribed a kid nearby to go for them, giving him sixty cents and saying, "Buy a dog for yourself at the same time."

A few minutes later, the kid came back with forty-five cents change and said, "They only had my hot dog left."

☺

"Life for a baseball bench warmer," says my good friend and personal manager, Bill Robbins, "is a many-splintered thing."

☺

When a Detroit baseball scout signed up a teen-age pitcher, the front office wired the lad to report immediately to the Tigers' farm club in Montgomery, Alabama. The following day the secretary received a collect call from the rookie. "Gee, Mr. Smith, do you mind if I don't report for another couple of days?" he pleaded.

"But why?" asked the surprised Smith.

"Because I haven't had time to make the collections on my paper route yet!"

☺

Speaking about pitchers, I heard of one who was sent to a psychiatrist by his manager who suspected a mental problem. The pitcher who had done extensive reading on muscle spasms mentioned a rare muscular disorder which he thought was the root of his trouble.

"Nonsense," protested the psychiatrist. "You wouldn't know whether you had that or not. With that ailment there's no discomfort of any kind."

"I know," gasped the pitcher. "My symptoms exactly."

☺

The baseball manager sought out his third baseman in the locker room. "Joe," he said, putting his arm around the player's shoulder, "it's all right if you forget all those batting tips I gave you. We just traded you to Kansas City."

☺

Fighters are very well-mannered people. Why? Because they always look out for the rights of others.

☺

In order to fill out the regimental boxing team, a GI was prevailed upon by his buddies to enter the divisional tournament. The soldier had never been in a fight in his life and looked forward to his initial bout with ill-concealed panic. When he came back to the barracks after the fight, he was in terrible shape; his head was both bloody and bowed.

"You poor guy," said the GI in the next bunk.

"That's not the half of it," gasped the boxer. "I gotta fight again tomorrow night. I won!"

☻

"Did you hear about the very pathetic fighter? He was on the mat so often he wore out his welcome.

☻

"My brother has a fortune in his own right."
"A coming millionaire?"
"No, a coming heavyweight champion!"

☻

"Hey Max," cried the first burglar, "let's get out of this place. We've broken into the home of the heavyweight champ."
"Don't worry," retorted the second burglar. "He won't fight for anything less than $100,000."

☻

A battered fighter was floored. The referee started the count over him, "One, two, three, four . . ." His manager shouted to him, "Don't get up 'til eight, don't get up 'til eight!" "Okay," the fighter replied. "What time is it now?"

☺

Speaking about floored fighters, how about the fellow who was knocked to the canvas midway in the third round? Although the punch which had downed him was a light one, he didn't get up until after the ten count.

"Whatsa matter, you crazy?" demanded his manager after the fight. "You wasn't hit hard. Whyncha get up in time?"

"I was so mad at being floored by that jerk," explained the defeated pug, "that I thought I'd better count to ten before I did anything."

☺

"Just think," said the conceited heavyweight boxer, "millions of people will watch me fight on TV tonight."

"Yes," retorted a boxing scribe, "and they'll all know the results at least ten seconds before you will."

☺

"Yes, sir," gloated the beaten fighter's trainer enthusiastically. "You really had him worried in the seventh round. He thought he'd killed you."

☺

A fighter was taking a terrific beating in the ring. When he stumbled back to his corner after the bell sounded, his manager looked at him briefly and said, "Let him hit ya with his left for a while. Your face is crooked."

☺

In a small fight club, the fans were disgusted with the lack of action in the ring. The two battlers did nothing but circle each other, with no punches being thrown. A forbidding silence mounted in the arena. Then . . . .

"Hit him now, ya bum," a spectator called. "You got the wind with yah!"

☺

Asked why he decided to give up fighting, an undefeated champion said, "I looked in the mirror after my last fight and saw my beaten up face and decided there must be an easier way to meet congenial people of my own age."

☺

"What did you think of the big fight last night, Mike?"

"Big fight! If my wife and I had a fight like that, the kids would boo us!"

☺

At a particularly dull fight at Madison Square Garden, an irate fan yelled, "Hey ref, put out the lights and let those bums go to sleep!"

"No, don't do that!" shouted another voice from ringside. "I'm reading."

☺

FIRST FIGHTER: When I hit a man, he remembers it.

SECOND FIGHTER: When I hit a man, he's through remembering.

☺

The slap-happy fighter reeled to his corner at the end of the fifth round. His face was badly battered.

"How'm I doin'?" he mumbled.

His manager patted him on the shoulder.

"Swell kid," he enthused. "You've got the other guy on the run."

"Yeah?" cried the fighter.

"Sure thing," nodded his manager. "But just make sure he doesn't catch you again."

☺

"How did you feel when you entered the ring?"

"It was just like going to bed."

"Like going to bed?"

"Yes, I took off my robe, climbed in, and in two minutes I was asleep."

☺

A real football fan is one who knows the nationality of every man on the All-American Team.

☺

My favorite football story concerns the college president who decided to lend a hand in the recruiting of new members for the team. He toured a number of school gridirons throughout the country. When he returned to his own campus, he called his coach.

"How did you make out?" asked the coach.

"Well, I saw one team that went through a 15-game schedule unbeaten, untied, and unscored on. The amusing thing about it is that their line averaged only 135, their backfield only 125, and they had no passer or kicker," reported the president.

"Well," said the coach. "I don't suppose you wasted any

scholarships on them?"

"No," replied the president, "but I hired their coach as your successor."

☺

"Winning isn't everything," says George DeWitt, "but no college football coach ever got a raise for building character during a season."

☺

A girl told her football-hero boy friend, "You've made me the happiest girl in the world tonight, Moose. You didn't wear your football shoes!"

☺

A big college halfback bumped into an elderly man in the Assembly Hall and shouted, "Hey Bud, why don't you watch where ya goin'?"

The man replied, "Look here, Sonny, I'll have you know I'm the football coach here."

"Gee, Coach, I'm sorry. I though you were only the principal."

☺

"Tell me, sir, why do the students cheer so loudly when a football player gets hurt?"

"That's so the ladies can't hear what he's saying."

☺

Calvin Haley of the TV Coffee Shop, heard a teacher ask her pupils to list, in their opinions, the eleven greatest Americans. As they were writing, she stopped at one desk. "Have you finished your list, Bobby?" she asked.

"Not quite," answered the boy. "I can't decide on the full-back."

☻

A football coach told his high school team, "And remember that football develops individuality, initiative, and leadership. Now get out there and do exactly as I tell you."

☻

"What would happen," a football expert was asked, "if a team was trying to kick the extra point, and the ball burst in the air with half going over the bar and half under it?"

"The way I see it," remarked the expert after thinking for a few moments, "the team would be out eighteen bucks."

☻

The story is told of the football game that was played on a Thanksgiving Day in Philadelphia. In the midst of a deluge of snow and rain, the Cornell captain won the toss and bitterly

stared out over Franklin Field covered with cold, gray slush.

"Do we have to play football in that fluid?" he demanded.

"Yes," was the implacable reply. "Which end you want?"

"Well," said the player, "we'll kick with the tide."

☺

An easterner on a tour of California stopped for lunch in a small town and noticing he was opposite a college, decided to take a look at the place. As he passed a sweater-clad student on the campus, he stopped the lad and asked the name of the school.

"Sorry, sir, I don't know," the lad replied. "I'm just a football player here."

☺

It had been a terrible season for the local football team, and a friend was trying to cheer up the coach.

"At least you've taught the boys fine sportsmanship," he comforted. "They're certainly good losers."

"Good," growled the coach. "Why, they're perfect!"

☺

A doctor, who was a prominent alumnus, was asked to give the boys a pep talk at a rally before the first football game of the season.

The doctor was most enthusiastic. Throughout the speech he interspersed the following statement:

"Give 'em hell boys! When you get in that game, you want to give 'em H-E-L-L."

The next speaker was a mild-mannered minister. He arose and in a small voice said, "Boys, give them what the doctor ordered."

☺

And then there was the guy who couldn't make up his mind whether to buy a ticket to the Army-Notre Dame game or a seat on the Stock Exchange. They were both the same price.

☺

"I used to play football and I carried the ball every play."
"Were you the star player?"
"No, but it was my ball."

☺

Anyone who has spent a day at the race track will tell you this: no horse can go as fast as the money you bet on him.

☺

Speaking about horses, I'm reminded of the story about the fellow who entered an eight-year-old in a race. Since the old horse had no previous races, the odds on him were 90 to 1. But when the race began, he tore down the track like a flash and wound up twelve lengths ahead of his closest competitor. The stewards were naturally suspicious and called the owner to their stand for questioning.

"How come you never raced this horse before?" they demanded. "After all, you've had him for eight years."

"Well, to tell the truth," the owner said sheepishly, "we couldn't catch him until he was seven."

☺

MOTHER: Violet, before you get serious with that boy friend of yours, be sure he is always kind and considerate.

VIOLET: Oh, I'm sure of that, Mother. Why, only the other day he put his shirt on a horse that was scratched.

☺

A bookie was testifying before the crime investigating committee to determine the honesty of horse racing. "The boss gave me $25,000 to fix the race," he said. "There were four other horses in the race and I gave each jockey $5,000 apiece."

"That's only $20,000," interjected a brilliant senator.

"I know," replied the bookie. "I needed the other $5,000 to fix the photographer in case of a photo finish."

☺

The horse had won the big race and was proudly telling his neighbor in the adjoining stall about it.

"And besides," added the winner happily, "I was promised, if I won the race, I'd get two extra bales of hay. And, brother, that ain't money."

☺

ED: Were you lucky at the races yesterday?

NED: I certainly was. I found a quarter after the last race so I didn't have to walk home.

☺

An enthusiastic racing fan made repeated trips to the ticket window to place his money on Take Courage in the last race. When he did so for the fourth time, a stranger tapped him on the shoulder.

"Excuse me," the stranger said. "It's none of my business, I guess, but if I were you, I wouldn't put all that money on Take Courage. He's not going to win."

"How can you tell?" asked the other.

"Well, if you must know," replied the stranger, "I own Take Courage, and I'm sure he's not going to win."

"In that case," was the response, "all I can say is that it's going to be a mighty slow race. I own the other four horses."

☺

At a racetrack some one asked a jockey, "How do you make a slow horse fast?"

"Don't feed him," replied the jockey.

☺

And then there was the horse who gave such a bad performance in his first race it made his parents turn over in their glue bottles.

☺

A sharpie sold a naive racing fan a broken-down filly. When the fan went to the stable to see his new purchase, he spotted a vet laboriously working over the horse.

"Is my horse sick?" asked the new owner.

"She's not the picture of health," the vet informed him, "but we hope to pull her through."

"Will I ever be able to race her?" asked the fan.

"Chances are you will," the vet assured him, "and you'll probably beat her, too."

☺

"Is horse racing a clean sport?"

"Well, it cleans quite a few every day."

☺

And before we leave this chapter, just remember this: it's easy to pick a winner at the track. Just don't take any money with you.

TALES OF SALESMEN

Mankind is divided into two classes; those who earn their living by the sweat of their brow and those who sell them handkerchiefs, cold drinks, and air conditioners. Selling is similar to hog-calling; it isn't the noise you make, it's the appeal in your voice. A good salesman, like a good cook, creates an appetite when the buyer doesn't seem hungry.

☺

Dick Nolan of the San Francisco *Examiner* likes this one:
Lost in the back roads of the Ozark countryside, the salesman slammed on the brakes and pulled his big car to a stop abreast of an elderly farmhand, trudging along in the broiling sun.

"Hey," he called, "can you give me directions to the next town?"

"Sure," said the farmhand, wiping his sweating brow. "You turn right at the next intersection, go about ten miles until you see a big barn, turn right again and go until you see a grocery store, then go right until you come to Carson's Corners. Then turn left."

Half an hour later, the same car came along the same road and drew up near the same farmhand, resting beside the road.

"I never could follow directions in strange country," said the driver. "Would you be kind enough to get in and point the way for me?"

"Yes," said the farmhand, climbing in. "Just go straight ahead. Sometimes I send you fellers around two or three times before you offer me a ride."

The story is told of a man who tried to buy a suit at one of those "walk-a-flight-and-save-a-dollar" establishments. One of the partners tried every suit but one on the customer. Each time the fellow put a suit on, the partner would turn him around and around so he could view himself in the mirror. Finally, the other partner took over, showed the customer one suit, and made a sale.

"You see how easy it was," he admonished. "I did it on the very first try!"

"I know," shrugged his partner, "but who made him dizzy?"

Sam Mandlebaum, my accountant, overheard this at the International:

Two traveling salesmen were discussing television.

"It ruined us," said one.

"I know," said the other. "Now the farmers get the newest jokes before we do."

A salesman I know uses the same routine every time he checks into a hotel. He casually tells the operator to get the White House on the phone. Then he asks to speak to the President. His second call is to the Vice-President.

"I never get them on the phone," he once told me, "but from then on, I'm always sure to receive great service at the hotel."

☺

Speaking about hotels, I like the yarn about the salesman who spent a week at a very exclusive one. On the day of his departure, he received a two-page itemized bill. When he looked it over, he recognized every item except the very last. It was a two-dollar charge for stationery.

"But I didn't use any stationery," he exclaimed, showing the bill to the clerk.

"The stationery referred to," exclaimed the clerk, "is the paper on which this bill is written!"

☺

The greatest salesman I ever heard of was the one who sold two milking machines to a farmer with one cow and then took the cow as a down payment.

☺

"Is Jim a good salesman?"

"Good salesman! Hah! The only orders he ever takes are from his wife."

☺

Dick Friendlich of the San Francisco *Chronicle* chuckled when I told him this one:

A salesman needed $35 for plane fare home, but all he had

was $25. He took his $25 to a pawn shop and hocked it for $20. Then he sold his pawn ticket to a passerby for $15, thereby giving him the $35 he needed.

☺

And Hal Shaefer, also of the San Francisco *Chronicle,* prefers this one:

The boss and his sales manager looked gloomily at the sales chart on the wall. In one corner was a graph showing the company's descending grosses. The rest of the chart contained a map of the territory, with pins stuck in it showing the location of the various salesmen.

"Frankly," the boss sighed, "I think we have only one hope. Let's take the pins out of the map and stick them in the salesmen."

☺

A salesmen always kept his hat on while working at his office desk. When kidded about it, he shot back, "That's to remind me I have no business being here."

☺

The sales clerk went to his boss and complained, "How," he asked, "can I stop women customers from complaining about our prices and talking about the low prices in the good old days?"

"It's simple," answered the head man. "Act surprised and tell them you didn't think they were old enough to remember them."

☺

A salesman, passing through Florida, bought a dozen coconuts and ordered the dealer to send them home to his wife. A month later, when he was passing through again, the salesman returned to the fellow's store and screamed, "I bought a dozen coconuts from you, and when I called my wife, she said she had only received ten."

"Don't get excited," soothed the dealer. "That's part of our service. Two were bad so we saved your wife the trouble of throwing them away."

☺

A sales manager was getting loaded in a bar because he had just been fired. He was asked what was wrong.

"Nothing," he explained. "I'm just drunk with no power."

☺

Robert Natella was a very imaginative fellow. Accordingly, he entered a used car showroom, browsed around a bit, and picked out the worst-looking car in the place.

The auto salesman, sensing that Robert might be attracted to a more flashy model, suggested that he look at some of the other autos on the floor.

"This one's the one I want," Robert insisted. "Of all the cars you have in this place, it's the one most likely to break down, isn't it?"

"Most likely to break down? Well, er, I guess so, but I don't understand?"

"It's like this," Robert explained. "When the car breaks down and a crowd gathers around me, I'll sell them my storm windows."

☺

A traveling salesman who was driving along one of those old Ozark dirt roads stopped in front of an old shack.

"How far is it to the nearest town?" he asked an old woman sitting in a rocking chair.

"Well, lemme see," she answered, scratching her head. "Pa

figures it's about ten miles goin' and about twelve miles comin'."

"What was that?" asked the salesman, obviously puzzled by her odd reply.

"Well, ya see," she explained. "Pa walks straighter goin' than comin'."

☺

TRAVELING SALESMAN: Good morning. Did you ever see anything as unsettled as the weather the last few days?

HOTEL MANAGER: Well, there's your bill here!

☺

Bob Blackburn of the Ottawa *Citizen* applauded when I told him this story:

A young salesman decided he was tired of working for others; so he went into business for himself. Later, a friend asked him how it was to be his own boss.

"I don't know," he replied. "The police won't let me park in front of my own premises; tax collectors tell me how to keep my books; my banker tells me how much balance I must maintain; transport contractors tell me how my goods must be packed; customers tell me how my goods must be made; and the Government tells me how to keep records in triplicate.

"And on top of that, I just got married."

☺

And Ottawa *Journal* scribe David McDonald laughed at this one:

The manager of a department store was mystified by the number of "No Sale" recordings rung up on the cash register by a new salesgirl. He asked her about it.

"Well," she said, "every time I had a customer who didn't

156

buy anything I pushed the 'No Sale' button. Isn't that what it's for?"

☺

First Salesman: Why don't you go on a vacation? Can't your office get along without you?

Second Salesman: That's what I don't want them to find out!

☺

The sales manager was praising the efficiency of his organization at a banquet.

"We're now making a sale every three minutes," he announced proudly.

"That's not enough," came a voice from the audience.

The speaker paid no attention to the rude interruption but went on to tell of the new sales promotion and direct-mail campaign which would insure a sale every minute and a half.

"That's still not enough," the voice repeated.

Enraged, the speaker singled out the man who had spoken and barked, "You interrupted me twice. Now I wish you'd explain your remark."

"Certainly," came the reply, "There's a sucker born every minute."

☺

A pullman porter gave a salesman special attention on a trip down South.

"What's the average tip that you get?" asked the salesman as he was leaving the train.

"An average one is usually two dollars," the porter said.

The salesman handed over two dollars and remarked that a

job on a pullman must be pretty lucrative.

"It's not so hot," the porter said. "This is the first average tip I've gotten in a couple of months."

☻

Tim Burke of the Ottawa *Journal* prefers this one:

A bartender, eyeing a tipsy salesman, remarked, "If he has one more for the road, he'll need a map to get to the door."

☻

The salesman crashed into the boss's office and screamed, "I want a bigger commission or *else!*"

"Or else, *what?*" sneered the boss.

"Or else I'll go back and work for the commission I'm getting."

☻

When a salesman's wife hauled him into divorce court on the grounds of being unfaithful, she named a comely young model as corespondent.

"Miss Smith," said the Judge to the model, "did you go to a hotel with the defendant?"

"Yes, I did," she replied sweetly, "but I couldn't help it. He deceived me."

"And how did he do that?"

"Well, he told the reception clerk that I was his wife!"

☻

A salesman, driving through Texas, overtook a young man running along the road. He stopped and invited the perspiring runner to get in.

"An emergency, I suppose?" the driver asked.

"No," puffed the young man. "I always run like this when I want a ride. It seldom fails."

☺

Sign on a California highway: THIS MAY BE THE JET AGE, BUT BROTHER YOU AIN'T DRIVING ONE YET!

☺

The salesman and his new blonde companion were enjoying a little dinner in a private room at a night club. As the meal neared its finish, he cleared his throat and said, "Honey, how about a little demitasse now?"

"I knew it, I knew it!" the blonde exploded. "I knew you weren't treating me this nice for nothing!"

☺

Jesse Berlly, who always manages the impossible Broadway ducats, heard this from a customer:

Two salesmen met one evening after work.

"I made some very valuable contacts today," the first told his friend.

To which his companion replied, "I didn't make any sales today, either."

☺

Did you hear about the fellow who stopped a woman on Broadway and told her, "You're the first white woman I've seen in six months."

"Where've you been," she inquired, "darkest Africa?"

"Nope, selling silk in Florida."

☺

A traveling salesman was showing a farmer a pair of pajamas.

"Glory be!" exclaimed the farmer. "What are those things for?"

"They're worn at night," explained the salesman. "Like to buy a pair?"

"Me?" said the farmer. "What for? Only place I go at nights is to bed."

☺

A traveling salesman, stuck in a small town with motor trouble, was a little leery about the abilities of the local mechanics.

However, having no other choice, he walked over to the nearest garage and watched one of the mechanics at work. He was amazed at the fellow's efficiency. He was really skillful. He changed the car's oil and didn't spill a drop. Before he touched the upholstery, he wiped off his hands thoroughly. He handled the steering wheel as carefully as a newborn baby. And when he pulled the car into the street, he was slow and cautious, making sure there were no cars driving by.

The salesman was truly impressed and approached another mechanic working nearby. "That fellow is a careful mechanic," he said. "He really takes pains when he works on a car."

Without looking up, the mechanic replied, "Why shouldn't he, that's his car!"

☺

A salesman, on a trip with his wife, stopped for breakfast at one of the hotels where he generally spent the night. He ordered pancakes.

When the waitress brought his order, he asked, "Where's my honey?"

"Oh," replied the waitress, "she left last week and got another job."

☺

A harassed salesman walked into the psychiatrist's office.

When he was couched, he said, "Doctor, I've really got a problem. I live in a lavish, new twenty-five-room house in the swankiest neighborhood in Westchester. It has a 40 x 70 pool, five acres of formal gardens, servants' quarters for eight, and a garage that will accommodate twelve cars. I also have a cabin cruiser that sleeps six, a summer home on Long Island, and a new plane . . . ."

"Just a minute," interrupted the headshrinker, "what has all this got to do with your problem?"

"Because, Doctor," the salesman replied, "even with commissions, I never make more than $75 a week."

☺

BOOK SALESMAN: This book will do half your work.
BUSINESSMAN: Good, I'll take two.

☺

A sales manager who had just returned from a tour of inspection of the firm's Sahara Desert branch was asked, "Is is true that there's a constant water problem out there and they're always short of it?"

"Well, put it this way," explained the sales manager. "There are times when it's so dry out there that when they mail a letter they attach the stamp with a paper clip."

☺

A company was having its annual dinner for the twenty-five-year employees, and the boss had stepped up to the refreshment stand. The sales manager, fortified by a few trips to the same stand, decided now was the time to hit the old man for a raise.

So he walked over to the boss, stuck out his chin figuratively, and stated bluntly, "Mr. Barker, I've worked so hard and so conscientiously I've ruined my health."

"I know you have, Marvin," the boss answered, and raising his glass, he said dramatically, "Here's to your health!"

☺

A salesman, who was dining in a restaurant with his latest flame, said, "If my doctor could see me with this champagne and caviar, he'd go crazy."

"Why, are you supposed to be on a diet?" the girl asked.

"It isn't that," the salesman said. "I owe him $500."

☺

A sales manager had one of his salesmen on the carpet. The

young salesman resented the call-down and becoming quite angry, said, "Don't talk to me that way. I take orders from no man!"

"Now we're getting somewhere," said the sales manager. "That's just what I'm raising hell about."

☺

A one-time salesman who had joined the police force returned from his first beat and told the desk sergeant, "I like this job. The hours are good. The pay is right, and the customer is always wrong."

☺

A traveling salesman stopped at a lonely farmhouse and asked for a night's lodging. The farmer agreed to put him up, but, as in all traveling salesman jokes, said that they were short of beds and he'd have to sleep with one of his daughters.

In the middle of the night the bedroom door crashed open, a flashlight swept over the bed, and the salesman found himself staring into the business end of a shotgun.

"Well," drawled the farmer, "worked again! This makes *five* daughters I've gotten off my hands this year!"

☺

A salesman was racing along Highway 96 at about 95 miles an hour. A motorcycle cop stopped him and growled, "Didn't you see the speed limit posted back there?"

"Why, yes," the autoist replied. "But I thought it said 96 miles per hour."

"Brother," the cop sighed. "I'm sure glad I caught you before you turned onto Highway 414."

☺

Two salesmen, Al and Bill, were discussing the fact that so many girls' names were the same as the names of cities.

"Florence, Italy."

"Helena, Montana."

"Elizabeth, New Jersey."

"Indianapolis, Indiana."

"Just a minute, Al. Indianapolis isn't a girl's name."

"Is that so? Do you know *everybody?*"

☺

SALESMAN FROM THE CITY: What's that strange odor?

FARMER: Fresh air.

☺

The secretary always knew her boss was a quick-thinking, go-getting salesman. But she never knew how sharp he really was until the phone rang in his real estate office and a soft female voice asked, "Do you sell maternity clothes?"

"No, madam," the boss replied, "but could we interest you in a larger house?"

☺

A salesman was trying to sell the young wife an egg-timer. "Your husband's eggs will be just right if you use this," he assured her.

"But I don't need it," she answered brightly. "My husband likes his eggs the way I do them. I just look through the window at the traffic lights and give them three reds and two greens."

☺

A salesman was driving through Kentucky when he noticed a man and his small daughter sitting beside a brook. The salesman stopped his car and approached the two. "You have a lovely little girl," he told the farmer. "What's her name?"

"Sybilistina," the farmer replied.

"That's a pretty long name," said the salesman.

"Look, mister," the farmer answered. "We're not city folks. We've got time."

☺

The live-wire salesman walked into the factory and demanded an interview with the manager.

"Look here, sir," he began energetically. "I'd like to talk to your men and sell them my correspondence course on how to put fire and sparkle into their work."

The manager turned pale.

"Get out of here," he roared. "Get out, you idiot. This is a dynamite factory."

☺

Two traveling salesmen met in the home office. "I hear you're going out West this trip," said one.

"Yep," said the other. "I'm really gonna take in the sights this trip."

"Be sure you see Old Faithful," said the first.

"See it?" moaned the second salesman. "I'm taking her with me."

☺

A door-to-door salesman stopped at a suburbanite's house one day. "I have something here," he said, "that will make you popular, make your life happier, and bring you a host of new friends."

"Good," said the suburbanite. "I'll take a fifth."

☺

A salesman, passing through a small town in the Ozarks, stopped for gas at a lonely filling station. On a hunch, he asked

the proprietor if he could buy some moonshine, too. After assuring himself that the salesman was no "revenooer," the proprietor came out with two jugs. "Got two kinds," he said. "Which kind do you want?"

"I don't understand," the salesman said. "What's the difference?"

"Plenty!" the mountain man cackled. "One's for courtin', other's fer fightin'."

☺

SALESMAN: This gravy is excellent. I must have the recipe.

WAITER: Sorry, sir, this restaurant is owned by a retired newspaper columnist. We never reveal our sauces.

☺

SALES MANAGER: I think it's a good time to sell the Joneses a car.

SALESMAN: What makes you think so?

SALES MANAGER: Their neighbor just bought a new one.

☻

A tombstone salesman and a widow were discussing the epitaph to be inscribed on her late husband's grave.

"How would a simple 'Gone Home' do?" asked the salesman.

"I think that would suit nicely," replied the widow. "It was always the last place he ever thought of going."

☻

A salesman, who was traveling through Ohio, stopped off at a diner for lunch. His bill was $1.45, and he paid it with a $2 bill. The waiter gave him a fifty-cent piece and a nickel. The salesman left the nickel and walked out with the half dollar.

"Well," sighed the waiter. "I gambled and I lost."

☻

A salesman who was deathly frightened of dentists got a terrific toothache while he was in Florida. He had always made it a habit to stay away as far as he could from dentists, but this time the pain was killing him. Accordingly, he went to a dentist, told him about the pain and also of his fear of dentists.

Being the sympathetic type, the dentist gave him a big shot of whiskey. The salesman swallowed it down in one gulp.

"Feel any braver now?" asked the dentist.

"Do I feel any braver?" snarled the salesman. "Brother, I'd like to see you try to mess with my teeth now."

☻

A salesman who stopped off to buy some blankets at an

Oklahoma Indian Reservation was introduced to an Indian family. "I'm Brave Eagle," said the oldest member. "This is my son, Fighting Bird, and this is my grandson, Jet Plane."

☺

"I don't like yes men," a sales manager warned his new assistant. "I want you to tell me what you really think, even if it costs you your job."

☺

A salesman was being interviewed by the personnel manager of a large industrial concern.

"What we are looking for," the personnel manager said, "is a man of vision, a man with drive, determination and courage, a man who never quits, who can inspire others—in short, a man who can pull the company's bowling team out of last place."

☺

Said one traveling salesman to another in a restaurant, "What's the matter, Max? You only had a sandwich for lunch. Usually you have a big meal. Are you on a diet?"

"No, on commission."

☺

Two salesmen were discussing a third. "He's probably the most conceited salesman who ever lived," said the first. "He's thoughtless, inconsiderate, and would do anything to make a sale. I guess you really don't know him as well as I do?"

"You're wrong," argued the other. "I think I know him every bit as well as you do."

"How could you possibly know him as well as I do?" snapped back the first. "I'm his best friend."

☺

168

A sales manager was stressing the importance of repetition to an employee. "When you're selling our product you must repeatedly praise its value because repetition is the most important factor in selling. Do you understand?"

"Yes, sir," replied the employee. "And now I'd like to ask you a question."

"What is it?"

"Can I get a raise, a raise, a raise?"

☻

"Did you ever do any public speaking?" asked the sales manager.

"Well," answered the candidate for the job, "I once proposed to a country girl on a party line."

☻

An insurance salesman was getting nowhere in his attempts to sell a policy to a farmer. "Look at it this way," he said finally. "How would your wife carry on if you should die?"

"Well," answered the farmer reasonably, "I don't reckon that's any concern o' mine so long as she behaves while I'm alive."

☻

"The cocktails on a salesman's expense account," says Phil Harris, "sometimes run into a staggering figure."

☻

A man went into a clothing store to buy a suit. The salesman asked him his name, age, religion, occupation, college, high school, hobbies, political party, and his wife's maiden name.

"Why all the questions?" the customer asked. "All I want is a suit."

"Sir, this is not just an ordinary tailor shop," the salesman said. "We don't merely sell you a suit. We find a suit that is exactly right for you.

"We make a study of your personality and your background and your surroundings. We send to the part of Australia that has the kind of sheep your character and mood require.

"We ship that particular blend of wool to London to be combed and sponged according to a special formula. Then the wool is woven in a section of Scotland where the climate is most favorable to your temperament. Then we fit and measure you carefully.

"Finally, after much careful thought and study, the suit is made. There are more fittings and more changes. And then . . ."

"Wait a minute," the customer said. "I need this suit tomorrow night for my nephew's wedding."

"Don't worry," the salesman said. "You'll have it."

☻

Jack Douglas says, "An insurance salesman sold me a retirement policy. If I keep up the payments for ten years, he can retire."

☻

JOE: I've been selling women's apparel for the last ten years.
MOE: Well, I'll bet you know all the tricks of the trade.
JOE: No, there's a blonde in Boston I never got to meet.

☻

A salesman from Ohio, stopping at a New York hotel during his first sales trip to the big city, called the switchboard to order a cab. Informed that "you don't call them—you just go down on the street and get one," he protested courteously that he had called cabs in Chicago, Detroit, and Los Angeles.

"You can in small towns," the operator interrupted, "but not in New York."

☺

"I've come back to buy that car you showed me yesterday," the man said as he stepped into the auto showroom.

"That's fine," the salesman said. "I thought you'd be back. Now, tell me what was the dominant feature that made you decide to buy this car?"

The man replied, "My wife."

☺

A salesman, stopping off at a Midwestern farm, became engrossed in conversation with a farmer. "I'm very excited," said the traveling man. "My son just won a college scholarship."

"I know just how you feel," said the farmer. "I felt the same way when my pig won a medal at the State Fair."

☺

The pretty young salesgirl who had recently been added to the vacuum cleaner company's door-to-door staff was reporting fantastic sales. The manager called her in for a word of commendation.

"What's your secret?" he asked affably.

"Simple," she replied. "I get the housewife's undivided attention because I always insist on talking to her husband. And I speak to him so softly, she strains to catch every word."

☺

Equally ingenious was the door-to-door salesman who developed an irresistible sales pitch.

When a housewife answered his ring, he would simply say,

"You should have seen what I saw at your neighbor's. May I come in?"

☻

"And remember, my friends," the lecturer told his audience. "There will be no buying and selling in Heaven."

"That," mumbled a salesman at a back table, "is not where business has gone."

☻

The salesman who returned from Florida described conditions there.

"In some parts of Miami, business is so bad that even people who don't intend to pay aren't buying."

☻

And before we leave this chapter, here's something for you to remember: few salesmen leave footprints in the sands of time, because they're too busy covering up their tracks.

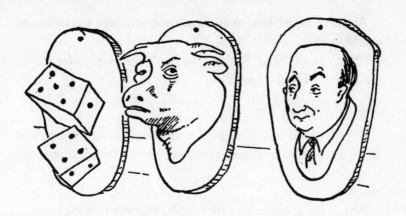

KATLEMAN'S KAPERS

If you've ever been to Las Vegas, you know that the El Rancho Vegas which is owned by Beldon Katleman is one of the most popular hotels in the gambling state.

Beldon is an extremely witty fellow and always comes up with clever quips.

I remember one time when a guest asked him what the biggest points of interest in Las Vegas were. Belden replied, "Seven and eleven."

On another occasion, a female guest who was worrying about her husband—he had spent seven straight nights losing a fortune playing blackjack—confronted Beldon and asked if her husband's behavior was more unusual than that of other guests. "I'll tell you what I tell everybody else," Beldon told her. "It's all right to play blackjack as long as you're having fun. But if you get angry, then it's gambling."

☺

A tourist asked Beldon if there were any race tracks in the gambling state.

"None at all," said Beldon. "In Las Vegas, we prefer to put the cards before the horse."

☺

A fellow who was spending his vacation in Las Vegas wired his sister: HAVING A WONDERFUL TIME. WISH I COULD AFFORD IT.

☺

WILL: I'm going to play dice, and I'm going to win.
PHIL: How to you know?
WILL: I feel it in my bones.

☺

A New Yorker, who had heard from a very unauthoritative source that it was simple to make a fortune at the gambling tables in Las Vegas, took a major portion of his life's savings and journeyed to the gambling state.

Upon arriving, he checked into a hotel and immediately went to the blackjack table where he bet $200. But the cards were bad and he lost. Then he decided to try his luck at the roulette table. He bet $500 on a number but once again lost. Disappointed, but not disillusioned, he next went to the dice tables. Feeling certain his luck would change, he bet his remaining $5,000. However, he lost again.

Completely busted, he went over to the desk clerk and borrowed money to call his wife in New York to forward some more money.

He stepped into the phone booth and told the operator the number he wanted.

"That will be $2.85, please," advised the operator.

He put the money in the coin box and waited for his number.

But, as luck would have it, he was connected with a Chinese laundry on 14th Street.

He immediately called the operator and told her of her error and asked for a refund.

"I'm sorry, sir," came the quick reply. "Your number lost again."

☺

A gambler's seven-year-old son, asked to count in kindergarten, came up with "1, 2, 3, 4, 5, 6, 7, 8, 9, 10, jack, queen, king."

☺

A guy was shooting dice at a Las Vegas Casino. He was doing pretty well when suddenly he felt a hand in his pocket. He grabbed it. Then he turned and found himself looking into a little guy's baby-blue eyes. "What are you doing?" he demanded.

"I'm just making change," the little guy alibied.

"Why don't you ask if you want to make change?"

The little guy said, "I never speak to strangers."

☺

A dishonest gambler complained, "I've got the hardest luck. Even when I'm cheating, I can't win."

☺

Gambling isn't the only thing Las Vegas is noted for. Anyone who's seen some of the shows put on at any of the night clubs on the famous "Vegas Strip" will tell you that pound for pound, Las Vegas probably has the prettiest chorus girls in the United States.

Most of these girls enjoy their work, but there are many who are looking to meet the right millionaire who will marry them and give them a life of ease.

I'm thinking specifically of one chorus girl who described her intended husband, a wealthy Midwest industrialist. "It's the little things about John that I like. He owns a small mansion, a small yacht, and a small racing stable."

☺

"I may have trouble finding the kind of husband I want," another said. "He'll have to be smart enough to make a huge sum of money but dumb enough to give it all to me."

☺

First Chorus Girl: When I refused to marry Bill, he said that he was going to take a trip around the world to forget.

Second Chorus Girl: So?

First Chorus Girl: So, I told him, if he had enough money for that, I would reconsider my refusal.

☺

A fellow had married a chorus girl who was one of a pair of identical twins. But within a year of his marriage, he found himself in a court of law applying to the judge on the bench for a divorce.

"But why do you want a divorce?" asked the judge.

"Well, it's this way," explained the guy. "My wife's twin sister lives with us, and I often come home and kiss her by mistake."

"But surely there is some difference between the two women," said the judge.

"You bet your life there is," exclaimed the husband. "That's why I want a divorce!"

☺

Jeanne Sager, who does my press relations, likes this story:

A beautiful chorus girl visited a psychiatrist. Before she was able to say a word, he said, "I know exactly what's bothering you. It's a man, isn't it?"

"Yes," she said. "He insists on kissing me every day of the week."

The psychiatrist told her to put her foot down and refuse.

The next day she returned and said, "Now he insists on hugging me."

The psychiatrist again told her to use her will power and refuse.

On the third day, she returned in an almost hysterical state. "What does he want now?" asked the psychiatrist.

"It's terrible," sobbed the chorus girl. "Now he wants a divorce."

☻

NED: There was a big killing in a dice game.
FRED: What happened?
NED: A guy shot seven.

☻

Shikey Toushin, who operates the Jewel Box at the Las Vegas Sands, likes the story about the theatrical agent who died and went to heaven where he noticed an angel playing a harp. He listened for a while and then tapped the angel on the shoulder.

"I like the way you play, son," he said, "but let me give you a tip. Take up the piano. There's no call for harpists these days."

☻

A rich Texan heard that one of the leading Las Vegas hotels was for sale and that he could get it for about ten million dollars. Accordingly, he sent a trusted agent to see about the deal with orders not to offer more than twelve million.

A few days later the agent phoned in.

"We can pick it up for eleven million, boss. But we're in trouble."

"How come?"

"They want a $2,500 down payment in cash!"

☺

"A Texan, a New Yorker, and a doctor played poker. The Texan held four kings and the New Yorker held five aces."

"What did the doctor hold?"

"An autopsy on the New Yorker's body."

☺

A TV producer was telling Beldon Katleman about a new idea he had for a quiz show.

"Each week," he explained, "we'll pick a new contestant and give him the answers to the questions."

"So?" said Beldon. "What's so unusual about that?"

"Plenty," the producer said. "The answers will be wrong."

☺

Two college professors, who were spending their Christmas vacations at the El Rancho, were seated in the lobby discussing the human body and the fact that it's 92 per cent water.

While they were in the course of discussion, a shapely member of the hotel's chorus line passed by. Conversation ceased for a moment as the professors studied her.

Then one remarked, "Boy, she sure did a lot with her 8 per cent."

☺

The fellows at the Friars swear they saw this sign on an elegant Cadillac: MADE IN LAS VEGAS THE HARD WAY!

☺

A chorus girl was having a difficult time finding a suitable man.

"You want too much of a man," a friend said.

"But all I'm looking for is a man who's kind and understand-

ing," exclaimed the chorus cutie. "Is that expecting too much of a millionaire?"

☺

Comic Larry Best says it was so crowded when he went to Las Vegas that he had to go to a psychiatrist to find a place to lie down.

☺

Houston columnist Paul Hochuli tells of the extremely sad-looking guy who was seated at the El Rancho Bar sipping his drink.

"Frank," asked a friend, "what in the world is the matter?"

"Oh, I'm having trouble with my wife," Frank explained.

"What happened?"

"Well, she told me she wasn't going to speak to me for thirty days."

"But," his friend objected, "that ought to make you happy."

"It did," Frank answered, "but today is the last day."

☺

A vacationing Hollywood agent was surprised when his waiter in a small Las Vegas restaurant tapped him on the arm and chuckled, "Remember me? I'll bet you're surprised to see me waiting on tables!"

"I'm not surprised at all," the agent remarked. "I remember your acting."

☺

A comic who was appearing at the El Rancho, walked into a psychiatrist's office and the psychiatrist told him to lie down and tell him everything. The comic did. So now, the psychiatrist is doing the comic's act in Miami.

☺

Four cardsharps got together and a tense, hard-fought contest ensued. Suddenly, the dealer tossed his cards down and said, "This game is crooked."

"What makes you think so?" queried the cardsharp on his left.

"I can tell," replied the dealer, "because you're not playing the same hand I dealt you."

☺

A forty-five-year-old bachelor complained to Beldon Katleman that no matter what girl he brought home as a potential bride, his mother expressed disapproval. Beldon advised him, "Find a girl just like your mother; then she's bound to like her."

A few months later the bachelor returned to the El Rancho and told Beldon, "I took your advice. I found a girl who looked like my mother, talked like her, and even cooked like her. My mother loved her."

"And did you marry her?" asked Beldon.

"No," said the guy.

"Why not?"

"Because my father hated her!"

☺

Marshall and William were dining in a Las Vegas restaurant when to Marshall's disgust, William calmly helped himself to the larger fish on the platter.

"Fine manners you've got, William," admonished Marshall. "If I'd been in your place, I'd have taken the smaller fish."

"Well," replied William with his mouth full, "you've got it!"

☺

A sales manager, attending a convention in Las Vegas, met a curvaceous chorine whom he found exceedingly appealing. Since he was a happily married man, he didn't know what to do.

Accordingly, he asked his boss, "I hate to appear bold like this, but I need your advice. Would you cheat on your wife?"

Shrugging his shoulders, the boss replied, "Who else—my mother-in-law?"

☺

While we're on the subject of "faithful" husbands, how about the Las Vegas hotel owner who, while returning from a trip to New York, went to his compartment and found two lovely girls there. Checking their tickets, the girls discovered that they had boarded the wrong train. Upset, they asked if they might remain in the compartment anyway.

The hotel owner carefully explained that he was a married man, one of the most famous hotel men in the country, a highly respected citizen of Las Vegas, and he couldn't afford the slightest touch of scandal.

"I'm sorry," he finished, "but one of you will have to leave."

☺

Another passenger on the same train, who had an upper berth, was making a general nuisance of himself.

"Hey, conductor," he cried out, "will you get me a glass of water, please?"

"My goodness," replied the exasperated conductor, "that's the tenth glass of water I've gotten you in the last five minutes. I never heard of anyone drinking so much water."

"I'm not drinking it," the passenger said. "My berth is on fire!"

☺

"You beast, you animal," cried the chorus cutie. "I'm going back to mother."

"Never mind," said the guy. "I'll go back to my wife."

☺

A gambler, just back from Las Vegas, told a friend he'd undergone "Las Vegas Surgery." "I had my wallet removed painlessly," he said.

☺

Joe E. Lewis, who is one of the country's leading night club comics, often headlines at the El Rancho Vegas. Joe E. is one of the best-loved entertainers in show business, and the stories about his ability to drink liquor are legendary. Joe has many theories about drinking, such as: "An alcoholic isn't always the guy who's had one drink too many. He's usually the guy who thinks he's had one too few."

When he was a young comic breaking into the business, Joe was once working in a night club in Chicago. The owner feared that Joe might get drunk and be unable to go on.

"Lewis," he warned, "the first time I catch you drinking, out you go."

Joe worked in the club for over a week and didn't touch a glass of whiskey. One night after his act, he returned to his dressing room and was greeted by the owner who was holding a half-full bottle of Scotch in his hand.

"I warned you, Joe," he said.

"But that's not my bottle," said Joe.

"Can you prove it?"

"I certainly can," said Joe. "If it were mine it wouldn't be half full!"

☺

Joe E. defines Alcoholics Anonymous as an organization that takes people apart to see what makes 'em hic.

One of his favorite drinking stories concerns the cop who asked a lush, "Where do you live?"

"Right here," came the reply. "I rang the bell, but nobody answered."

"How long ago was that?" asked the cop.

"Oh, a couple of hours ago."

"Well, why don't you try ringing again?"

"Aw, the heck with them," said the drunk. "Let 'em wait."

☺

Joe E. claims you can always spot an alcoholic at a cocktail party. He's the guy who's talking to the bartender.

☺

Not all of Joe's stories deal with liquor. He often tells the tale of the local wolf who was seen at a night club with the wife of one of his best friends.

"For Pete's sake," said a friend of both, "have you no pride? Why, she's the wife of one of your brother lodge members!"

"Yeah, I know," replied the wolf calmly, "but he isn't in good standing."

☺

Another of his favorites deals with the concert violinist who had had very few engagements of late, who found it both discouraging and disturbing to see a particularly unskilled street violinist attract a shower of coins and bills every time he appeared in the neighborhood.

Not only did the passersby stop to put money in the itinerant fiddler's hat, but windows opened and envelopes of money snowed down on his miserable instrument.

"Maybe there's something to this," thought the concert violinist. And in desperation, he took his Stradivarius to another part of town and played his heart out on a street corner. He had never played so beautifully, but he collected not one red cent.

Next time the virtuoso saw the street musician, he stopped to talk to him. "How does it happen," he asked, "that with your unskilled playing you still collect so much money?"

"Simple," replied the other, "I also happen to be a bookie."

☺

"Why do you always win at cards and lose at races?"
"Because I can't keep a horse up my sleeve."

☺

Dallas columnist Tony Zoppi reports he overheard a Las Vegas chorus girl tell a friend, "What I'm looking for is a man who will treat me as if I were a voter and he was a candidate."

☺

"Bill went to Las Vegas to get away from it all."
"He did?"
"Yes, but unfortunately, it all got away from him."

☺

And before we end this chapter, just remember this: in Las Vegas or anywhere else, the only safe bet is the one you forget to make.

HOORAY FOR THE IRISH

One of the most rewarding experiences I've had as a comedian occurred last year when I was completing an engagement at Blinstrub's in Boston. On what was supposed to be the last night of my engagement, Stanley Blinstrub, the owner, had sold out the club to the St. Joseph's Guild which was holding a testimonial dinner for one of its members.

Since the Guild was composed entirely of Irishmen, Stanley thought it might be a good idea if I ended my date a day earlier and let Jimmy Joyce replace me. Jimmy is a talented young comic who's very popular in Boston where he's called the "Irish Myron Cohen."

However, being the gentleman that he is, Stanley never said a word to me. But somehow I sensed his uneasiness and felt obligated to discuss the matter with him. When I broached the subject, Stanley pointed out that Jimmy was very popular with the Irish and might feel more at home with the Guild than I would. I assured him that I had no qualms about entertaining the Guild.

I always found the Irish to be a wonderful group of people, blessed with a fine sense of humor and a rich lore.

When I stepped on the stage that night, I remembered that they called Jimmy Joyce "The Irish Myron Cohen." To break the ice, I simply said, "Good evening ladies and gentlemen. My name is Myron Cohen, but I'm also known as "The Jewish Jimmy Joyce."

The audience loved this opening and for the rest of the evening they were on my side.

☺

One of my favorite Irish stories was told to me by my good friend Sister Mary Augustine of the Marist Missions, and deals with the pretty Irish lass who fell in love with a fellow who hadn't been to church in fifteen years.

"You're not a bad fellow, Pat," the girl's father told the suitor, "but before you marry my daughter, you'll have to become a good Catholic."

The suitor agreed and began spending a great deal of his time reading about Catholicism and discussing religion with the local priest.

For the next six months, he studied and learned everything he could about the religion. During this time, he never missed a Sunday in church.

Finally, one day, the girl approached her father and, with a tear in her eye, said, "Father, Pat isn't going to marry me."

Slightly confused, her father said, "I don't understand. He seemed like he'd developed a real interest in religion. What happened? Why the sudden change?"

"He hasn't changed, Father," said the girl.

"Then why aren't you getting married?" asked her father, more confused than ever.

"Because, Father, Pat has become so interested in Catholicism that he's decided to become a priest."

☻

An American staying in London was introduced to an Irishman who asked him, "And what country do you belong to?"

"The greatest country in the world," replied the American.

"So do I," replied the Irishman. "But where's your brogue?"

☻

A priest was writing the certificate at a christening but couldn't remember the date.

Looking to the mother of the baby he said, "This is the 16th, isn't it, Mrs. Flynn?"

"Oh, no, Father," said Mrs. Flynn. "This is only the 9th I've had."

☻

Pat and Mike were talking:

"Being that it's St. Patrick's Day, I'd like to bring home a special treat for my family," said Pat.

"I would, also," said Mike. "Let's walk down the street, and as soon as we see a butcher shop, we'll go in and buy some nice juicy steaks."

They began walking, and in a couple of minutes, they came to a butcher store.

"Let's go in," said Pat.

"Faith and begorra, Pat," said Mike. "Can't you see what the sign on that window says—KOSHER MEAT MARKET!"

"So it does," said Pat. "Say, Mike, I've seen that sign on lots of windows. Just between you and me, what does it mean?"

"Well, Pat," explained Mike, "to you that sign means nothing, and to me that sign means nothing. But for the Jewish people—that's Duncan Hines."

☻

A rich Texan, who was visiting Ireland, became engrossed in conversation with a native.

"Ireland isn't a bad country," said the Texan, "but it doesn't compare to Texas."

"Do you know that a man can get on a train in Texas early Monday morning, have his breakfast, have his lunch, have his supper, and then go to sleep. When he gets up Tuesday morning, he's still on the same train, and he can have his breakfast, have his lunch, have his supper, and go to bed again. And do you know that when he gets up Wednesday morning and gets off that train, he's still in Texas?"

"So what's so unusual about that?" said the Irishman. "We have slow trains in Ireland also."

☻

Back in the days when Brooklyn had a baseball team, Francis Cardinal Spellman was watching a World Series game at Ebbets Field. During the course of the game, a high foul was hit toward his box seat. Catcher Roy Campanella tried to reach it but missed, and the ball hit the Cardinal's knee. Campanella quickly asked whether he had been hurt.

"Don't worry about it, Roy," the Cardinal said. "A priest's knees are the toughest part of his anatomy."

☻

A priest and a rabbi were making plans for an interfaith luncheon.

"We can serve pork and beans," said the priest.

"Good idea," said the rabbi, "and we'll hold it on a Friday."

☻

A hungry Irishman went into a restaurant on Friday and asked the waiter, "Have you any lobster?"

"No."

"Have you any shrimp?"

"No."

"All right," said the Irishman, "then bring me a steak smothered with onions. The Lord knows I asked for fish."

☻

"I hear you went to the ballgame last Sunday instead of to church."

"That's a lie. And I've got the fish to prove it."

☻

Joe McCarthy, of the American Weekly, tells of the monastery where the monks were allowed to speak aloud on only one day of the year. And on that day only one monk was permitted to say anything.

One year, on the appointed day, the monk whose turn it was to talk stood up and said, "I hate the mashed potatoes we have here. They're always lumpy."

Having spoken, he sat down and lapsed into silence again. Another year passed by, until the day for talking came once more. Another monk arose and said, "I like the mashed potatoes. I think they're delicious. In fact I can hardly wait for the night when we have mashed potatoes."

Again silence for twelve months, while summer turned into autumn and winter gave way to spring. Finally, the day arrived when a third monk was allowed to speak.

"I want a transfer to another monastery," he said. "I can't stand this constant bickering!"

☺

Boston *American* columnist Alan Frazer tells of the Irishman who was stopped by a friend as he was about to enter a bar.

"Stay out of that place, Mike," warned his friend. "If you go in, the devil goes in with you."

"If he does," said Mike, "he pays for his own drinks."

☺

"The Irish are the best fighters in the world," announced Tim Connor. "They can lick anyone in the world."

"Oh, they're not such good fighters," said a Swede. "Me and my brothers Ole, Nels, and Sven Petersen and two other fellows, we licked one of them yesterday."

☺

A parishioner, who hadn't attended church all summer, met the priest one afternoon.

"Hello, Fred," greeted the priest. "I haven't seen you for a long time. In fact, I don't believe you've been to church since last May."

"Has it been that long?"

"Yes, Fred. I believe it has."

"Well, Father," said Fred, "I'll tell you the reason why. When it's hot, you can't expect people to sit in a church. Nowadays, everything is air conditioned—movies, offices, restaurants. And churches should be, too. Otherwise, attendance will drop."

"Well," said the priest, "one place has been without air conditioning for ages, and I understand attendance is holding up well there."

☻

"Abstinence," said Father Murphy, "is a wonderful thing, Tom."

"Sure, and it is, Father," said Tom, "if practiced in moderation."

☻

Did you hear about the Irish psychiatrist who used a Murphy bed instead of a couch?

☻

Irishmen are not against taking a drink now and then and Irish lore is such that many of its legendary tales—especially those concerning liquor—have been so distorted by time that they have almost reached the point of complete absurdity.

Mr. Donegan caught the bartender at Casey's bar in an unguarded moment and begged, "Pat, my mother-in-law has gone to her reward, and it's a ten spot I'm needin' for a wreath to uphold the Donegan standards. Can you advance me the ten?"

The bartender emptied his pockets and the cash register but the total came to $9.30.

"That'll do," said Donegan hastily. "I'll take the other seventy cents in drinks."

☺

KEVIN: If you take another drink, you'll hate yourself in the morning.

SEAN: So what! I'll sleep late.

☺

"St. Patrick's Day," according to Nick Kenny of the New York *Mirror,* "is a day on which the Irish march up Fifth Avenue and stagger down Sixth Avenue."

☺

Bennett Cerf tells of the O'Connel brothers who were dining in a strange restaurant. As usual, they had too much to drink. Near the end of the meal, brother Tim decided he wanted to wash up and asked the waiter where the washroom was. He was directed to a door to the left of the elevator.

"Go down two steps, and there you are," said the waiter. Being slightly inebriated, Tim unfortunately did not have full control of his faculties and forgot to turn to the left. He opened the elevator door, took one step, and promptly fell down the shaft.

The O'Connels came from hardy stock, and Tim was merely stunned. When his brother Mike rose to wash up, however, Tim cautioned him.

"Look out for that second step, Mike. It's a son-of-a-gun!"

☺

"Every time I see you," screamed Sullivan's wife, "you have a bottle in your pocket."

Sullivan replied, "You don't expect me to keep it in my mouth all the time, do you?"

☺

O'Leary was selling tickets for a church benefit to a friend.

The friend said, "I'm sorry I can't buy one. I won't be able to attend, but my spirit will be there with you."

"Good," said O'Leary. "I have a $2, a $3, and a $5 ticket. Where would you like your spirit to sit?"

☺

George Clarke, the Boston *Record* columnist, chuckled when I told him the tale of Pat McCoy who approached the minister who had married him just five minutes before and said, "How much do I owe you?"

The minister smiled, "As much as you think the girl's worth."

Pat handed him a dollar which the minister took without comment. Pat was reluctant to leave; in fact, the minister thought he wasn't going to get rid of the couple.

"Have I forgotten anything?" he finally asked.

"Yes," said Pat. "My change."

☺

A wealthy farmer decided to go to church one Sunday. After services he approached the preacher with much enthusiasm. "Reverend," he said, "that was a damned good sermon you gave, damned good!"

"I'm happy you liked it," said the reverend, "but I wish you wouldn't use those terms in expressing yourself."

"I can't help it, Reverend. I still think it was a damned good sermon," said the farmer. "In fact, I was so impressed that I put a hundred-dollar bill in the collection basket."

The reverend replied, "The hell you did!"

☺

And speaking about Satan's domain, Jim O'Connor, of the New York *Journal-American,* tells of the old Irishman who became so sick that a priest was sent for to administer last rites. But, somehow, the man recovered, and in a couple of weeks was hobbling about as good as ever.

"Ah, Dennis," said the priest, "it's a sight for sore eyes to be seeing you up again. I thought you were a goner for sure. You had a bad, bad time of it."

"Yes," agreed Dennis. "I certainly did."

"When you were at death's door," questioned the priest, "how did you feel? Were you afraid to meet your Maker?"

"I wasn't worrying about that so much," replied Dennis. "It was the other gentleman I wasn't anxious to meet."

☺

If I tell any more Irish stories, they'll start calling me the LepreCohen so maybe I'd better end this chapter now.

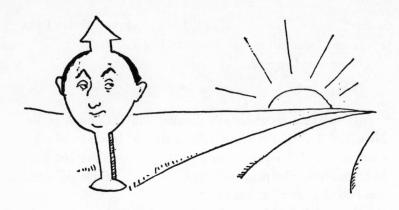

ONE FOR THE ROAD

When I went from Garment Center salesman to night club comedian, many of my friends were amazed by the relative ease with which I made the switch. They didn't realize how similar these fields really are.

The salesman's customer is his audience. He must "make friends" much in the same way the comedian establishes a rapport with his listeners. The salesman borrows even further from the comedian in that he often relies on a humorous story to break ground. Also, both are concerned with the appropriateness of his material—the comedian fits his routine to the audience while the salesman chooses just the right story for each customer.

In my salesman days, I once had a customer named Max who had three lovely children he was always bragging about. Max had more pictures of his kids in his wallet than the Rogue's Gallery has in its files. Whenever I went to see him, stories like these often helped me make a sale.

☺

Young Bob picked up some extra allowance money by cutting the neighbor's lawns on Saturday. One Saturday morning, Bob Senior noticed that Junior was leaving a bit later than usual. He asked his son why he wasn't getting an early start.

"I found out, Dad," was the reply, "that I get more work from people who are already halfway through."

☺

Mother and daughter were in the kitchen washing dishes while father and seven-year-old Billy were in the living room. Suddenly father and son heard a crash of falling dishes. They listened expectantly.

"It was Mother," Billy finally announced.

"How do you know?" father asked.

"Because," answered Billy firmly, "she isn't saying anything."

☺

A little boy came home dejectedly from his first day of school and announced, "I'm not going tomorrow."

"Why not?" questioned his mother.

"Well, I can't read, I can't write, and teacher won't let me talk. So what's the use?"

☺

A mother, riding on a train, looked up from her magazine and frowned. "No, I don't know the name of that station where we just stopped. Why do you ask?"

"Because Sister got off there," her small son replied.

☺

"My son is certainly a smart kid. He's only four, and he can already spell his name frontwards and backwards."

"What's his name?"

"Otto."

☺

Nine-year-old Michael Mason, who brought home a terrible report card asked his father, "What do you think the trouble with me is, Dad, heredity or environment?"

☺

A fellow was trying to fix a door that didn't hang right.

"Hey, son," he called to his boy, "get me a screwdriver, will you please?"

After what seemed like a terribly long time, the youngster came back and said apologetically, "Gee, Dad, I've got the orange juice, but I can't find the vodka."

☺

TEACHER: This essay on "Our Dog" is exactly the same as your brother's.

JOHNNY: Yes ma'am. It's the same dog.

☺

A Hollywood producer's son received a very unusual report card. Instead of the customary "Poor," "Fair," "Good," and "Excellent," it was marked "Sensational," "Magnificent," "Stupendous," and "Colossal."

☺

George Q. Lewis, Executive Director of the Gagwriters' Association of America, met a friend whose wife had recently given birth to their first child.

"Can he talk yet?" asked George.

The proud father replied, "What's the sense of his learning to talk when he gets everything by yelling?"

☻

A six-year-old came home from school one day and told his father, "Daddy, my teacher takes a great interest in you."

"How do you know?" asked his father.

"Today, she told me to sit down and behave five times, and then she said she wondered what kind of a father I had."

☻

A boy in the same class came home from school and told his mother, "My teacher is mean but fair!"

"What do you mean—mean but fair?" questioned his mother.

"She's mean to everybody."

☻

The harassed mother took her incorrigible son to see a psychiatrist after every other disciplinary method had failed.

"What seems to be the trouble?" asked the medical man. "Does he feel insecure?"

"I don't know," replied the mother, "but everyone else in the neighborhood certainly does."

☻

I had another customer whose son was a doctor. When I visited him, I always came with a fresh supply of doctor stories:

The officious new nurse was determined to show her authority on her first day on the job. When a man walked into the office, she ordered him to step into the next room and undress.

"But I only want my sore throat checked," he protested.

It made no difference. Without listening further, she again ordered him into the next room. There he found another man undressing, and again he complained that he was merely a throat patient.

"What are you complaining about?" asked the other man. "I'm the doctor!"

☺

My physician of long standing, William Hitzig, passed this one along to me:

A fellow consulted a doctor because he wasn't feeling well. "Do you smoke excessively?" asked the M.D.

"No."

"Drink a lot?"

"No."

"Keep late hours?"

"Nope."

The doctor shook his head and asked, "How can I cure you if you have nothing to give up?"

☺

DOCTOR: There's nothing wrong with you. All you need is a little sun and air.

PATIENT: I guess you're right, but my wife is dead set against having children.

☺

The doctor at the Army base had a young corporal as his assistant to keep track of the paper work. The young man was curious about the doctor's affairs. He was always asking questions and one morning said, "In civilian life were many of your cases accidents?"

"I don't know," the doctor replied.

"How come you don't know?" the corporal asked.

"Soldier," the doctor replied, "I was an obstetrician."

☺

A woman decided to have the shape of her nose altered.

"How much will you charge?" she asked a plastic surgeon.

"Five thousand dollars."

"Five thousand dollars! Isn't there something less expensive?"

"Well," replied the surgeon, "you could try walking into a lamp post."

☻

The Mayo Clinic has worked out some extremely effective diets. One time an irritable millionaire patient was given one of these diets to follow. He looked it over with an angry eye and then snarled at Dr. Mayo, "Why do you doctors order a fellow to cut out just the things he likes?"

"Because," Mayo answered, "he never eats or drinks the things he doesn't like so it stands to reason it must be the things he does like that are disagreeing with him."

☻

A bum entered a doctor's office. He looked worried.

"Doctor," he said, "you've got to help me. I swallowed a silver dollar about five years ago."

"Good heavens, man!" screamed the doctor. "Why have you waited five years? Why didn't you go to a doctor the day you swallowed the silver dollar?"

"To tell the truth," replied the bum, "I didn't need the money at the time."

☻

"How is the patient's mental attitude?" asked the doctor.

"Much improved," answered the night nurse. "He has stopped praying for his recovery and started praying for your bill to be reasonable."

☻

A doctor stepped into the patient's room. Five minutes later he came out and asked for a corkscrew. Then he went back to his patient. In another five minutes, he was out again, and this time asked for a screwdriver. Soon after, he came out again and demanded a chisel and hammer. The distraught husband couldn't stand it any longer. He pleaded, "For heaven's sake, doctor, what's wrong with my wife?"

"I don't know yet," the medic replied. "I can't get my bag open."

☺

I once knew a woman buyer who spent a good portion of her spare time reading about the Hollywood stars in movie magazines. She knew everything about everybody in Hollywood and appreciated stories about filmdom.

A young dancer began her career in show business by getting a job as a chorus girl. Her salary was $75 a week.

When she began working, she noticed that her neighbors suddenly began acting cool toward her. The woman next door spoke to her crossly about her parents' home and how it needed a paint job and a new roof. The man across the street made remarks about daughters who were too selfish to provide their elders with new cars and vacation trips. Puzzled, the girl spoke to her father about it.

"Oh don't worry," her father said, laughing. "I've been telling everybody you're making $5,000 a week."

☺

A movie director was trying to impress a young actress with the importance of making a good entrance.

"When you enter the room," he told her, "I want every man in the audience to drop his popcorn."

☺

A Hollywood producer had just completed a real dull motion picture—a regular "bomb." It cost five million dollars and ran more than five hours. The producer was desperate. As a last resort, he called in six top Hollywood writers. He screened the

movie for them, hoping that one could come up with the magic suggestion to save the film.

The long, monotonous screening finished and the producer jumped to his feet and addressed the writers.

"Well," he said, "you saw it. Now, are there any suggestions?"

After several moments of painful silence, one writer announced, "I have a suggestion. I think this film should be cut."

Grasping at any straw, the producer said quickly, "Okay, where?"

"Right up the middle!"

☺

A Hollywood producer, while in the midst of producing an historic film about Abe Lincoln, decided that the film was dragging. He turned to his head writer and said, "I want you to find out if Lincoln ever knew any girl who remotely resembled Marilyn Monroe."

☺

The Hollywood producer received a story entitled, "The Optimist." He called his staff together and said, "Boys, this title must be changed to something simpler. We all know what an optimist is, but how many other people know it's an eye doctor?"

☺

The story is told of the film star who was disappointed at not being asked to make a speech on the occasion of his retirement.

"What makes it really heartbreaking," he told an associate, "is that I spent five hours in the make-up department having a lump put in my throat."

☺

A noted actor was asked if he was going to allow his two-year-old son to go on the stage.

"Not for another year," he replied. "I want him to lead a normal childhood."

☺

A singer had several auditions with a talent agent and each time sang the same song.

"Tell me," the agent asked, "why do you always sing the same song?"

The singer replied, "Because it haunts me."

"It's no wonder," said the agent. "You're continually murdering it."

☺

The movie usher was visiting a dentist. "Now, Bill," asked the dentist, "which tooth is bothering you?"

"The second from the left in the balcony!"

☺

In Hollywood, a censor phoned a studio official about some stills showing a girl in a rather revealing costume.

"They're okay if that's an evening gown," said the censor, "but if it's a nightgown, the picture's out!"

☺

A famed movie queen applying for a visa came to the blank: Single——Married——Divorced——. She hesitated a moment, then wrote, "Everything."

☺

In a little Midwestern town, there's a sign that proudly proclaims it to be the birthplace of a famous movie star. "Tell me," said a tourist to the gas station attendant, "does the great star ever visit this town with his wife?"

"Seven times, ma'am," replied the attendant. "And seven prettier women you've never seen."

☺

When a salesman meets a new customer, he obviously doesn't know anything about the customer's background and his likes and dislikes.

In my salesman days, when I was confronted with these situations, I resorted to general topics which are appealing to everyone. For instance, auto stories:

A nouveau riche manufacturer took an extended trip through Europe.

When he returned, he had a large gathering at his home

and displayed all his souvenirs to his guests.

"Tell me, Ralph," one of his friends asked, "did you bring back a Van Gogh or a Picasso?"

"Oh, no," replied Ralph, "they're all left-hand drive in Europe. Besides, I've got two Cadillacs already."

☺

Paul Bruun, of the Miami Beach *Florida Sun,* tells of the prominent manufacturer who had just completed a big business deal and was thinking of his good fortune while he was crossing a busy intersection. He appeared oblivious to everything going on around him and was looking up at the sky.

A motorist passed by and narrowly missed him.

"Hey, you!" screamed the fellow behind the wheel. "If you don't look where you're going, you'll go where you're looking!"

☺

EXAMINER: When a woman puts her hand out what does it mean?

APPLICANT: It means that she's either going to make a right or left turn, or go straight through, or stop.

☺

"Why do you have MDO 448 tattooed in reverse on your back?" a doctor asked his patient.

"That's not a tattoo. That's where my wife ran into me while I was opening the garage doors."

☺

One afternoon a rickety old car drew up to an exclusive café. The driver stepped up to a man lounging nearby and asked, "Will you keep an eye on my car while I make a phone call?" The other agreed.

When the driver returned, he asked the man how much he owed.

"Fifty dollars," was the reply.

"But that's robbery! I was only gone five minutes."

"I know," the man answered. "But it wasn't the time, it was the embarrassment. Everyone thought the car was mine."

☺

A woman, trying to back her car into a parking space, smashed into the car behind. Failing at this, she pulled out of the space, and while pulling in again, she banged into the car in front. Disgusted, she recklessly pulled out of the space and struck a passing car.

A cop who was watching approached her.

"Can I see your license, ma'am?" he asked politely.

"Oh don't be silly, officer," she replied quickly. "Who would give me a license?"

☺

Herb Kelly, of the Miami *News*, tells of Boris Smolovich who came to this country from his native Poland. After being passed by the immigration officials, he took up residence in Detroit because he heard that it was easy to get work there. Sure enough, he managed to find himself a well-paying job in an automobile factory.

After his first day of work, his curious wife was anxious to learn what sort of work Boris did at the plant.

"I have a good job," he informed her. "I work on an assembly line."

"What does that mean?" she asked.

"Well," explained Boris, "I work in a unit with three other fellows. It's like a team. When a car comes down the line, the first fellow puts on the bolts, the second fellow attaches the washer, and third fellow holds both in place."

"Yes, but what do *you* do?"

"Me," answered Boris proudly. "I screw up the works."

☺

"If all the autoists were laid end to end," says comic Danny Davis, "ninety-eight percent of them would immediately pull out of line and try to pass the car in front."

☺

George Bourke, of the Miami *Herald,* observes, "It takes 1,875 bolts and screws to put an auto together, but it takes only one nut to scatter it all over the road."

☺

Psychiatrist stories have a general appeal.

After months of analysis, a patient was told that he was cured.

"You'll no longer have delusions of grandeur and imagine that you're Napoleon," his psychiatrist told him.

"That's wonderful," enthused the patient as he picked up the phone. "The first thing I'm going to do is call Josephine and tell her the good news!"

☺

"So," nodded the headshrinker to a new patient, "you think you're a dog. That is a very dangerous hallucination. How long have you been subject to it?"

"Ever since I was a puppy."

☺

A man visited a psychiatrist and told him that he'd developed the habit of making long-distance calls to himself. "Lately it's gotten worse," he said. "They're transatlantic calls, and it's costing me a fortune."

The dome doctor thought for a moment and then said, "Why not try reversing the charges?"

☺

A mother visited a psychiatrist and said, "I'm worried about my daughter because she's too fond of rock 'n roll music to have any other serious interests."

"There's a simple solution," said the psychiatrist. "All you have to do is buy some classical recordings. By taking advantage of her natural love for music, you can subtly channelize her in another direction."

A week later the mother returned and said, "I did what you told me."

"What happened?" asked the psychiatrist.

"I now have the only house in the neighborhood where they rock 'n roll to Chopin's 'Polonaise.'"

☺

A woman went to the psychiatrist and told him, "I'm awfully worried. I constantly talk to myself."

"That's not unsual," consoled the headshrinker. "Millions of normal people talk to themselves."

"I know," moaned the lady, "but you don't understand how much of a pest I can be."

☺

An advertising executive told a psychiatrist, "Doctor, I have never lost an account, and I've never had an ulcer. Also, I've never worn a gray flannel or three-button suit."

"I don't understand. What seems to be your problem?"

The ad man said, "Tell me, doctor, am I normal?"

☺

A distraught mother pleaded with a psychiatrist, "You must help my son. He spends all day making mud pies and when he gets done he tries to eat them."

"That's not unusual," soothed the psychiatrist. "Lots of boys make mud pies and try to eat them."

"I'm not so sure about that," replied the mother, "and neither is his wife!"

☺

A man visited a psychiatrist and told him, "You must help me. I have my entire ceiling and all the walls of my bedroom covered with pictures of Brigitte Bardot."

"I don't understand what your problem is," the psychiatrist said.

"My problem," said the patient, "is that I sleep on my stomach."

☺

A nurse rushed into a busy psychiatrist's office and exclaimed, "There's a man outside who claims he has a dual personality. What should I do?"

"Just tell him," replied the psychiatrist, "to go chase himself."

☺

"Doc," said the fellow to his headshrinker, "can you please cure me of snoring? I snore so loud that I continually keep waking myself up."

"If I were you," the psychiatrist advised, "I'd sleep in another room."

☺

Army stories, too, appeal to everyone.

A hoity-toity, second lieutenant was caught without proper

change in front of a cigarette machine. Accordingly, he flagged down a passing private and asked, "Got change of a dollar?"

"I think so," said the private cheerfully. "Wait till I see."

The lieutenant drew himself up stiffly and barked, "Private, that is not the way to address an officer. We'll replay this scene. Got change of a dollar?"

The private saluted smartly and said, "No, sir."

☺

It was near the end of World War II, and a German soldier, whose regiment was almost completely annihilated, approached his commanding officer and asked if he could take his long over-due furlough.

"I can't give you a furlough, Fritz," said the officer, "but maybe we can retreat through your home town."

☺

SERGEANT: What was your occupation before entering the army?

ROOKIE: Traveling salesman, sir.

SERGEANT: Stick around; you'll get plenty of orders here.

☺

A young soldier at Fort Dix was asked by his buddies how he had learned to take army discipline so readily.

"I'm used to it," he said. "My mother was an officer in the WAC."

☺

Two veterans were boasting about their old outfits.

"Why, our company was so well drilled," said one, "that, when we presented arms, all you could hear was slap, slap, click."

"Pretty fair," said the other. "But when our company presented arms, you could hear slap, slap, jingle."

"Jingle?" said the other. "What did that?"

"Oh, just our medals."

☺

SERGEANT: What is the first thing to do when cleaning a rifle?

PRIVATE: Look at the number.

SERGEANT: And what has that to do with it?

PRIVATE: To make sure I'm cleaning my own gun.

☺

A G.I., caught in his first barrage in a foxhole in Korea, found himself subjected to a sudden onset of hiccups. "Do me a favor, will you?" he implored his buddy. "Do something to scare me."

☺

My English cousins, Mildred and Julian Rose, tell of a British colonel visiting a United States military post, who got into a discussion with one of the officers as to which army had the better discipline. As the American was speaking, a private came in.

"Cap," he said, "I've got me a heavy date tonight. Can I use your jeep?"

"Sure," replied the captain. Then, turning to the colonel, he said, "There's proof of our discipline. He needn't have asked me."

☺

At a press luncheon in Washington, Major John Eisenhower recalled an incident during World War II, when, as second lieutenant and aide to his father, he was sent with a message to a colonel in the front line.

"My dad says to watch your right flank," the younger Eisenhower told the colonel.

"Fine," replied the puzzled officer, "and what does your mommy say?"

☺

Two soldiers were digging a trench. It was a very hot day, and both felt pretty tired.

"Do you remember the big poster saying, 'Enlist and See the World,'" asked one.

"Yes," replied his companion, "but why?"

"Well, I didn't know we had to dig clear through in order to see it."

☺

A general and a captain were walking down the street. They met many privates, and each time the captain would salute, he would mutter, "The same to you."

The general's curiosity soon get the better of him, and he asked, "Why do you always say that?"

The captain replied, "I was once a private, and I know what they are thinking."

☺

And best of all, the salesman can never go wrong by telling a story about himself.

I like the one about the traveling saleman who was driving through upstate New York when it began to pour. Soon, the visibility became so poor that he couldn't see five feet in front of him. As he was riding, he spotted a farmhouse and pulled into the driveway. He jumped out of the car, raced to the house, and knocked on the door.

In a few moments, the farmer appeared at the window,

spotted the salesman, and quickly opened the door.

"Come on in, young feller," he replied. "It's kinda wet out there."

When the salesman was inside, the farmer told him to sit by the fire and warm himself. Then he got the salesman a towel and made him a cup of hot tea.

After he was warm and dry, the salesman went to the window and looked out. It was still pouring. Turning to the farmer, he said, "It's awful outside. It would be treacherous to drive. Do you think you could put me up for the night?"

"I guess so," said the farmer, "but there's one thing I gotta tell you first."

"What is it?" asked the salesman.

"I ain't got a daughter."

"What!" screamed the salesman, as he picked up his hat and coat and raced to the door. "Of all the nerve . . . to think that I would stay with a farmer who didn't. How far is the next farm-house?"

☺

In a similar vein, Miami *Herald* columnist Jack Kofoed tells of the salesman who stopped at a farmhouse and asked the farmer, "Do you have a daughter?"

"Yup, and a real pretty one, too."

"Good," said the salesman. "I'll stay here for the night."

The next morning the salesman got up, packed his bag, and started to leave. As he was walking to his car, he spotted the farmer. "You old liar, you," he yelled. "I thought you said you had a daughter."

"I do," said the farmer.

"Don't lie to me," hollered the salesman, getting madder by the moment. "I was here all last night, and I didn't see her once. Did you ever hear of a traveling salesman who stayed in a farmhouse for a whole night without seeing the farmer's daughter?"

"There's a simple explanation," said the farmer.

"What is it?"

"My daughter is away at college."

☺

A salesman and his wife arrived in Europe on a combined business and pleasure trip. Tired and hungry from the long trip, the husband ordered a large meal.

His wife made some rapid calculations, then complained, "Jim, that adds up to about eight thousand calories."

"Who cares?" demanded Jim. "I'll put 'em on my expense account."

☺

The least popular salesman in the company was leaving and one of his co-workers was trying to get others in the office to give him a farewell dinner.

"Look," he told the other members of the staff, "it'll be a good feed, and we'll all have a lot of fun. We're even planning to award door prizes. One of you might win."

"Nothing doing," snapped one of the group. "I'd rather give that crumb a good swift kick where it would do the most good!"

"Hey!" exclaimed the party promoter. "How did you know? That's first prize!"

☺

A salesman who had been on one of the greatest selling sprees of his career accumulated a small fortune in commissions. Accordingly, he took an apartment on Park Avenue and spent his newly found wealth buying furnishings for it. He even built a garden on the roof. To accomplish this, tons of earth had to be hauled up.

Soon after the garden had been completed, it belatedly came to the attention of the owner of the building.

"What have you done?" he wailed to the salesman. "This roof cannot sustain such a weight. It will collapse."

"Are you sure?" asked the salesman.

"Of course, I'm sure. Now what are you going to do about it?"

"I'm going to move of course!" retorted the salesman. "You don't expect me to live in an unsafe building, do you?"

☺

My secretary, Ellie Malisoff, found this one very funny:

A salesman in trying to sell a refrigerator pleaded, "Lady, you can save enough on your food bill to pay for it."

"We're paying for a car on the carfare we save, and we're paying for a washing machine on the laundry bill we save. It looks like we just can't afford to save any more at the present time."

☺

A salesman, according to Herb Rau of the Miami *News*, is a man who, when right, must always keep his temper and when wrong must never lose it.

The story is told of the salesman who was waiting for a train when a stranger approached and asked him the time. The salesman, ordinarily accessible, ignored him. The stranger repeated the request, but the salesman continued to ignore him. A few minutes later, the stranger walked away.

A friend of the salesman, who was standing nearby, came over and asked, "Al, that was a perfectly reasonable request. Why didn't you tell the guy what time it was?"

"Listen," explained the salesman. "I'm standing here minding my own business. This guy wants to know what time it is. So, maybe I tell him. Then what? We get to talking, and this guy says, 'How about a drink?' So, we have a drink. Then, maybe we have some more drinks. After a while I say, 'How about coming up to my house for a bite to eat?' So, we go up to my house. We're eating sandwiches when my daughter who's twenty-one and very pretty comes in. She's a very sweet and attractive girl. So, she falls for the guy and this guy falls for her. Then, they get married. And any guy who can't afford a watch—well, I just don't want him in my family."

Speaking about time, my publisher informs me it's time to end this book.

Oddly, I find it more difficult to end a book than to begin one. When I begin, I'm full of enthusiasm because I'm getting another opportunity to share some of my favorite stories with an audience. But when I come to the end, I feel regretful because no one book, or even two, can hold all the wonderful stories I'd like to tell you.

I do hope you enjoyed these stories as much as I did telling them to you. I'm looking forward to seeing you soon in night clubs and on TV.

As my closing line, I'd like to expound this bit of philosophy: may you laugh as long as you live and live as long as you laugh.